Pierre-Joseph Buchoz

The toilet of Flora

A collection of the most simple and approved methods of preparing baths

Pierre-Joseph Buchoz

The toilet of Flora
A collection of the most simple and approved methods of preparing baths

ISBN/EAN: 9783337197766

Printed in Europe, USA, Canada, Australia, Japan

Cover: Foto ©Andreas Hilbeck / pixelio.de

More available books at **www.hansebooks.com**

THE

TOILET

OF

LORA.

The Graces.

THE

TOILET of FLORA;

OR,

A COLLECTION

OF THE

MOST SIMPLE AND APPROVED

METHODS of PREPARING

BATHS,	PERFUMES,
ESSENCES,	AND
POMATUMS,	SWEET-SCENTED
POWDERS,	WATERS.

WITH

RECEIPTS for COSMETICS of every Kind, that can fmooth and brighten the SKIN, give Force to BEAUTY, and take off the Appearance of OLD AGE and DECAY.

FOR THE USE OF THE LADIES.

A NEW EITION, IMPROVED.

LONDON,

Printed for J. MURRAY, No. 32, Fleet-ftreet; and W. NICOLL, St. Paul's Church Yard.

MDCCLXXIX.

ADVERTISEMENT.

THE chief Intention of this Performance is to point out, and explain to the Fair Sex, the Methods by which they may preferve and add to their Charms; and by which many natural Blemifhes and Imperfections may be remedied or concealed. The fame Share of Grace and Attractions is not poffeff-ed by all of them; but while the Improvement of their Perfons is the indifpenfable Duty of thofe who have

been

ADVERTISEMENT.

been little favoured by Nature, it
fhould not be neglected even by the
few who have received the largeft
Proportion of her Gifts. The fame
Art which will communicate to the
former the Power of pleafing, will
enable the latter to extend the Em-
pire of their Beauty. It is poffible
to remove, or, at leaft, to cover the
Defects of the one Clafs, and to
give Force and Luftre to the Perfec-
tions of the other.

The Author, however, though in
general he has framed his Work for
the Advantage of the Ladies, has
not entirely confined to it them. The
Virtues of Plants and Vegetables,
befide the Service they furnifh for
the

the Toilet, have their Ufe in Articles of Luxury. He has thence been induced to addrefs himfelf alfo to the Perfumer : and his Publication, he flatters himfelf, while it comprizes a very perfect Collection of the Methods which tend to improve Beauty, to repair the Waftes of Fatigue, and to avert the Marks of Age or Decline, includes likewife a full Account of whatever relates to domeftic Oeconomy and Expence.

Uncommon Pains have been taken to improve the prefent Edition, which contains a Syftem of the Cofmetic Art, infinitely fuperior to any that has hitherto appeared ; and it has likewife uniformly rendered the various Pre-

fcriptions

ADVERTISEMENT.

scriptions not only compatible with,
but subservient to, the Preservation,
and even the Improvement of Health;
an Object of the greatest Importance
in a Work of this Kind.

CONTENTS.

A 5

CONTENTS.

CONTENTS.

WATERS.

A 6

CONTENTS.

C O N T E N T S.

CONTENTS.

GLOVES.

BREATH.

OILS.

ESSENTIAL OILS, or QUINT-ESSENCES.

CONTENTS.

CONTENTS.

PERFUMES.

PASTILS.

PASTES.

POMATUMS.

CONTENTS.

POWDERS.

C O N T E N T S.

F L E A S.

W R I N K L E S.

C A R M I N E S.

CONTENTS.

SWEET SCENTED BAGS.

WASH-BALLS.

EYE-BROWS.

CONTENTS.

MARKS OF THE SKIN.

COMPLEXION.

WARTS.

VINEGARS.

CONTENTS.

EYES.

SUPPLEMENT.

USEFUL RECEIPTS.

CONTENTS.

CONTENTS.

DIFFERENT WAYS OF PREPARING SNUFF.

THE

THE

T O I L E T

OF

F L O R A.

No. 1. *An Aromatic Bath.*

BOIL, for the fpace of two or three minutes, in a fufficient quantity of river-water, one or more of the following plants; viz. Laurel, Thyme, Rofemary, Wild Thyme, Sweet-Marjoram, Baftard-Marjoram, Lavender, Southernwood, Wormwood, Sage, Pennyroyal, Sweet-Bafil, Balm, Wild Mint, Hyffop, Clove-july-flowers, Anife, Fennel, or any other herbs that have an agreeable fcent. Hav-

B

ing

ing ftrained off the liquor from the herbs, add to it a little Brandy, or camphorated Spirits of Wine.

This is an excellent bath to ftrengthen the limbs; it removes pains proceeding from cold, and promotes perfpiration.

2.   *A Cofmetic Bath.*

TAKE two pounds of Barley or Bean-meal, eight pounds of Bran, and a few handfuls of Borrage Leaves.   Boil thefe ingredients in a fufficient quantity of fpring water.   Nothing cleanfes and foftens the fkin like this bath.

3.   *An Emollient Bath for the Feet.*

BOIL, in water, a pound of Bran, with a few Marfh-mallow Roots, and two or three handfuls of Mallow Leaves.

4. *An Aromatic Bath for the Feet.*

TAKE four handfuls of Pennyroyal, Sage, and Rofemary, three handfuls of Angelica, and four ounces of Juniper Berries; boil thefe ingredients in a fufficient quantity of water, and ftrain off the liquor for ufe.

5. *An excellent Prefervative Balfam againſt the Plague.*

SCRAPE fine twelve Scorzonera and Goatſbread Roots; fimmer them over a gentle fire in three quarts of Lifbon or French White Wine, in a veffel clofely covered, to prevent the too great evaporation of the vinous fpirit. When the roots are fufficiently boiled, ftrain off the liquor through a linen ftrainer with a gentle preffure: then add to it the Juice of twelve Lemons, with Cloves, Gin-

ger,

ger, Cardamom Seeds, and Aloes Wood, grofsly powdered, of each half an ounce; and about one ounce of each of the following herbs, viz. frefh Leaves of Rue, Elder, Bramble, and Sage; boil all together over a gentle fire, till one quart is wafted away; ftrain the liquor off immediately through a ftrong linen bag, and keep it in an earthen or glafs veffel clofe ftopped. Drink every morning fafting, for nine days together, half a pint of this Balfam, by which means you will be able to refift the malignancy of the Atmofphere, though you even vifit infected perfons. The fame end may be promoted by wafhing the mouth and noftrils with Vinegar; and by holding to the nofe a bit of Camphire, flightly wrapped in muflin; or by frequently chewing a piece of Gum Myrrh.

6. *An excellent Cosmetic for the Face.*

TAKE a pound of levigated Hartshorn, two pounds of Rice Powder, half a pound of Cerufs, Powder of dried Bones, Frank-incenfe, Gum Maftic, and Gum Arabic, of each two ounces. Diffolve the whole in a fufficient quantity of Rofe-water, and wafh the face with this fluid.

7. *A curious Perfume.*

BOIL, in two quarts of Rofe-water, an ounce of Storax, and two ounces of Gum Benjamin; to which add, tied up in a piece of gauze or thin muflin, fix Cloves bruifed, half a drachm of Labdanum, as much Calamus Aromaticus, and a little Lemon-peel. Cover the veffel up clofe, and keep the ingredients boiling a great while: ftrain off the liquor without ftrong preffure, and let it ftand till it depofit the fediment, which keep for ufe in a box.

B 3

8. *Perfumed Chaplets and Medals.*

TAKE Marechal Powder, and make it into a paste with Mucilage of Gum Tragacanth and Arabic, prepared with All-flower-water (the receipt for which is contained in this book.) The mould into which it is put must be rubbed with a little Essence of Jassmine, or of any other sweet-scented herb, to prevent the Paste from sticking. This Paste in colour resembles Coffee.

9. *Receipt to thicken the Hair, and make it grow on a bald part.*

TAKE Roots of a Maiden Vine, Roots of Hemp, and Cores of soft Cabbages, of each two handfuls; dry and burn them; afterwards make a lye with the ashes. The head is to be washed with this lye three days successively, the part having been previously well rubbed with Honey.

10. *An approved Depilatory, or a Fluid for taking off the Hair.*

Take Polypody of the Oak, cut into very fmall pieces; put them into a glafs veffel, and pour on them as much Lifbon, or French White Wine, as will rife about an inch above the ingredients: digeft in balneo Mariæ (or a bath of hot water) for twenty-four hours; then diftil off the liquor by the heat of boiling water, till the whole has come over the helm. A linen cloth wetted with with this fluid, may be applied to the part on which the hair grows, and kept on it all night; repeating the application periodically till the hair falls off.

The diftilled water of the Leaves and Roots of Celandine, applied in the fame manner, has the like effect,

11. *A Powder to prevent Baldness.*

POWDER your head with powdered Parsley Seed, at night, once in three or four months, and the hair will never fall off.

12. *To quicken the Growth of Hair.*

DIP the teeth of your comb every morning in the expressed Juice of Nettles, and comb the hair the wrong way. This expedient will surprisingly quicken the growth of the hair.

Some, after having shaved the head, foment it with a decoction of Wormwood, Southernwood, Sage, Betony, Vervain, Marjoram, Myrtle, Roses, Dill, Rosemary, or Misletoe.

13. *A compound Oil for the same Intention.*

TAKE half a pound of green Southernwood bruised, boil it in a pint and a half
of

of Sweet Oil, and half a pint of Red Wine; when fufficiently boiled, remove it from the fire, and ftrain off the liquor through a linen bag: repeat this operation three times with frefh Southernwood. The laft time add to the ftrained liquor two ounces of Bears-greafe.

This oil quickly makes the hair fhoot out.

14. *A Fluid to make the Hair grow.*

TAKE the tops of Hemp as foon as the plant begins to appear above ground, and infufe them four and twenty hours in water. Dip the teeth of the comb in this fluid, and it will certainly quicken the growth of the hair.

25. *A Liniment of the fame Kind.*

TAKE fix drachms of Labdanum, two ounces of Bears-greafe, half an ounce of

Honey,

Honey, three drachms of powdered Southernwood, a drachm and a half of Afhes
of Calamus Aromaticus Roots, three
drachms of Balfam of Peru, and a little
Oil of Sweet Almonds. Mix into a liniment.

16. *To change the Colour of the Hair.*

FISRT wafh your head with fpring-
water, then dip your comb in Oil of
Tartar, and comb yourfelf in the Sun:
repeat this operation three times a day,
and at the end of eight days at moft the
hair will turn black. If you are defirous
of giving the hair a fine fcent, moiften it
with Oil of Benjamin.

17. *Simple Means of producing the fame Effect.*

THE Leaves of the Wild Vine change
the hairs black, and prevent their falling
off.

off. Burnt Cork; Roots of the Holm-oak, and Caper-tree; Barks of Willow, Walnut-tree and Pomegranate; Leaves of Artichoaks, the Mulberry-tree, Fig-tree, Rafberry-bufh; Shells of Beans; Gall and Cyprefs-nuts; Leaves of Myrtle; green Shells of Walnuts; Ivy-berries, Cockle, and red Beet-feeds, Poppy-flowers, Alum, and moft preparations of Lead. Thefe ingredients may be boiled in Rain-water, Wine or Vinegar, with the addition of fome cephalic Plant, as Sage, Marjoram, Balm, Betony, Clove-july-flowers, Laurel, &c. &c.

18. *To change the Hair or Beard black.*

TAKE Oil of Coftus and Myrtle, of each an ounce and a half; mix them well in a leaden mortar; adding liquid Pitch, exprefted Juice of Walnut Leaves and Laudanum, of each half an ounce; Gall-nuts, Black-lead, and Frankincenfe, of

B 6 each

each a drachm; and a sufficient quantity
of Mucilage of Gum Arabic made with a
decoction of Gall Nuts.

Rub the head and chin with this mixture, after they have been shaved.

19. *A Fluid to die the Hair of a flaxen Colour.*

TAKE a quart of Lye prepared from
the Ashes of Vine Twigs; Briony, Celandine Roots, and Turmeric, of each
half an ounce; Saffron and Lily Roots,
of each two drachms; Flowers of Mullein,
Yellow Stechas, Broom, and St. John's-
wort, of each a drachm; boil these ingredients together, and strain off the Liquor clear.

Frequently wash the hair with this fluid,
and in a little time it will change to a beautiful flaxen colour.

20. *A perfumed Basket.*

PLACE a layer of perfumed Cotton extremely thin and even on a piece of Taffety stretched in a frame; strew on it some Violet Powder, and then some Cyprefs Powder; cover the whole with another piece of Taffety : nothing more remains to complete the work, but to quilt it, and cut it of the fize of the basket, trimming the edges with ribband.

2. *Natural Cosmetics.*

THE Juice that iffues from the Birch-Tree, when wounded with an auger in fpring, is deterfive and excellent to clear the complexion : the fame virtue is attributed to its diftilled water. Some people recommend Strawberry-water; others the decoction of Orpiment, and fome Frog-fpawn-water.

22. *A remedy for Corns on the Feet.*

ROAST a Clove of Garlic, or an Onion, on a live coal or in hot aſhes; apply it to the corn, and faſten it on with a piece of cloth. This foftens the corn to fuch a degree, as to loofen and wholly remove it in two or three days. Foment the corn every other night in warm water, after which renew the application.

The fame intention will be yet more effectually anfwered by applying to the corn a bit of the plafter of Diachylon with the Gums, fpread on a fmall piece of linen; removing it occafionally to foment the corn with warm water, and pare off the foftened part with a penknife.

23. *A Coral Stick for the Teeth.*

MAKE a ftiff Pafte with Tooth Powder and a fufficient quantity of Mucilage of Gum

Gum Tragacanth : form with this Paſte little cylindrical Rollers, the thickneſs of a large gooſe quill, and about three inches in length. Dry them in the ſhade. The method of uſing this ſtick is to rub it againſt the teeth, which become cleaner in proportion as it waſtes.

24. *A receipt to clean the Teeth and Gums, and make the Fleſh grow cloſe to the Root of the Enamel.*

TAKE an ounce of Myrrh in fine powder, two ſpoonfuls of the beſt white Honey, and a little green Sage in fine powder; mix them well together, and rub the teeth and gums with a little of this Balſam every night and morning.

25. *Ditto, to ſtrengthen the Gums and faſten looſe Teeth.*

DISSOLVE an ounce of Myrrh as much as poſſible in half a pint of Red Wine and the ſame

same quantity of Oil of Almonds : Wash the mouth with this fluid every morning.

This is also an excellent remedy against worms in the teeth.

26. *Another.*

Dissolve a drachm of Cachoe (an Indian perfume) in a quart of Red Wine, and use it for washing the mouth.

27. *Or rather.*

Bruise Tobacco Roots in a mortar, and rub the teeth and gums with a linen cloth dipped in the Juice. You may also put some Tobacco bruised between the fingers into the hollow of the tooth. Or take the green Leaves of a Plum-tree, or of Rosemary, and boil them in Lees of Wine or Vinegar; gargle the mouth with the Wine as hot as you can bear it, and repeat it frequently.

28. *For rotten Teeth.*

MAKE a balfam with a fufficient quantity of Honey, two fcruples of Myrrh in
fine powder, a fcruple of Gum Juniper,
and ten grains of Roch Alum. Frequently apply this mixture to the decayed
tooth.

29. *A liquid Remedy for decayed Teeth.*

TAKE a pint of the Juice of the Wild
Gourd, a quarter of a pound of Mulberry
Bark, and Pellitory of Spain, each three
ounces; Roch Alum, Sal Gem, and Borax,
of each half an ounce. Put thefe ingredients into a glafs veffel, and diftill in a
fand heat to drynefs; take of this liquor
and Brandy, each an equal part, and wafh
the mouth with them warm. This mixture removes all putridity, and cleanfes
away dead flefh.

30. *A Powder to clean the Teeth.*

TAKE Dragon's Blood and Cinnamon, of each one ounce and a half, Burnt Alum, or Cream of Tartar, one ounce; beat all together into a very fine powder, and rub a little on the teeth every other day.

31. *A Remedy for sore Gums and loose Teeth.*

BOIL Oak Leaves in spring-water, and add to the decoction a few drops of Spirit of Sulphur. Gargle the mouth with a little of this liquor every morning while neceffary.

32. *An approved Receipt against that trouble-some Complaint, called the Teeth set on Edge.*

PURSLAIN, Sorrel, Sweet or Bitter Almonds, Walnuts, or burnt Bread, chewed, will certainly remove this disagreeable fenfation.

33. *A Liquid for cleansing the Teeth.*

TAKE Lemon Juice, two ounces, Burnt Alum and Salt, of each fix grains; boil them together about a minute in a glazed pipkin, and then ftrain through a linen cloth. The method of application is to wrap a bit of clean rag round the end of a ftick, dipping it in the Liquid, and rub it gently againft the teeth. You muft be careful not to have too much of the Liquid on the rag, for fear it fhould excoriate the gums or infide of the mouth. This application ought not to be ufed above once every two or three months.

34. *A fure Prefervative from the Tooth Ache, and Defluxions on the Gums or Teeth.*

AFTER having wafhed your mouth with water, as cleanlinefs and indeed health requires, you fhould every morning rince the mouth

mouth with a tea fpoonful of Lavender-Water mixed with an equal quantity of warm or cold water, whichever you like beft, to diminifh its activity. This fimple and innocent remedy is a certain prefervative, the fuccefs of which has been confirmed by long experience.

35. *A Method to make the Teeth beautifully white.*

TAKE Gum Tragacanth, one ounce; Pumice-ftone, two drachms; Gum Arabic, half an ounce; and Cryftals of Tartar, finely powdered, one ounce; diffolve the Gums in Rofe-water, and adding to it the powder, form the whole into little fticks, which are to be dried flowly in the fhade, and afterwards kept for ufe.

36. *Or,*

TAKE dried Leaves of Hyffop, Wild Thyme, and Mint, of each half an ounce;

Roch-

Roch Alum, prepared Hartſhorn, and Salt,
of each a drachm; calcine theſe ingredients
together in a pot placed on burning coals;
when ſufficiently calcined, add of Pepper
and Maſtic, each half a drachm, and of
Myrrh a ſcruple; reduce the whole into a
fine powder, and make them into a proper
conſiſtence with Storax diſſolved in Roſe-
water.　Rub the teeth with a ſmall bit of
this Mixture every morning, and afterwards waſh the mouth with warm Wine.

37. *Or,*

DIP a piece of clean rag in Vinegar of
Squills, and rub the teeth and gums with
it. This not only whitens, but faſtens and
ſtrengthens the roots of the teeth, and corrects an offenſive breath.

38. *Or,*

TAKE Roſe-water, Syrup of Violets,
clarified Honey, and Plantain-water, of
each

each half an ounce; Spirit of Vitriol one ounce; mix them together. Rub the teeth with a linen rag moistened in this Liquor, and then rince the mouth with equal parts of Rose and Plantain-water.

39. Or,

Rub them well with Nettle or Tobacco Ashes, or rather with Vine Ashes mixed with a little Honey.

40. *A Powder to cleanse the Teeth.*

Take prepared Coral and Dragons-blood, of each an ounce; Cinnamon and Cloves, of each six drachms; Cuttle-bone, and calcined Egg-shells, of each half an ounce; Sea Salt decrepitated, a drachm, all in fine powder: mix them in a marble mortar.

41. *The following was communicated by Mr. Rae, Surgeon Dentift, in the Adelphi, London.*

TAKE of Cuttlefifh-bone, and the fineft prepared Chalk, each half an ounce; Peruvian Bark, and Florentine Iris Root, each two drachms: reduce the whole into a fine Powder, and mix them. This may be coloured with a little Rofe Pink, and fcented with a few drops of Oil of Cinnamon.

42. *Or,*

TAKE Pumice-ftone prepared, Sealed Earth, and Red Coral prepared, of each an ounce; Dragons-blood, half an ounce; Cream of Tartar, an ounce and a half; Cinnamon, a quarter of an ounce; and Cloves, a fcruple: beat the whole together into a Powder.

This

This Powder ferves to cleanfe, whiten, and preferve the Teeth; and prevents the accidents that arife from the collection of Tartar or any other foulnefs about them.

43. *An efficacious Tooth-Powder.*

TAKE Myrrh, Roch Allum, Dragon's Blood, and Cream of Tartar, of each half an ounce; Mufk, two grains; and make them into a very fine powder. This, though fimple, is an efficacious dentifrice; but nothing of this kind fhould be applied too frequently to the teeth for fear of hurting the enamel.

44. *A Powder to cleanfe the Teeth.*

TAKE Pumice-Stone and Cuttle-fifh Bone, of each half an ounce; Tartar vitriolated, and Maftich, of each a drachm; Oil of Rhodium four drops: mix all into a fine powder.

45. *A Tincture to strengthen the Gums and prevent the Scurvy.*

TAKE an ounce of Peruvian Bark grofsly powdered, infuse it a fortnight or longer in half a pint of Brandy. Gargle the mouth every night or morning, with a tea fpoonful of this Tincture diluted with an equal quantity of Rofe-water.

46. *Manner of preparing the Roots for cleaning the Teeth, according to Mr. Baumè.*

THE roots that are ufed to clean the teeth are formed at both ends like little brufhes; and in all probability were fubftituted in the room of Tooth-brufhes, on account of their being fofter to the gums and more convenient. They are ufed in the following manner; one of the ends is moiftened with a little water, dipped into the Tooth-Powder, and then rubbed againft

C   the

the teeth till they look white. Fibrous
and woody Roots are beft formed into little brufhes, and on this account deferve a
preference to others. The Roots are de-
prived of their juicy parts by boiling them
feveral times in a large quantity of frefh
Water. When Lucern Roots are ufed,
thofe of two years growth are chofen, about
the thicknefs of one's little finger; fuch as
are thicker, unfound or worm-eaten, being
rejected. They are cut into pieces about
fix inches long, and, as we have juft ob-
ferved, are boiled in water till all the juicy
parts are extracted. Being then taken out,
they are left to drain; after which each
end of the roots is flit with a penknife
into the form of a little brufh, and they are
flowly dried to prevent their fplitting. In
the fame manner are prepared Liquorice
Roots. Marfh-mallow Roots are prepared
in an eafier way; but, on account of the

muci-

mucilage they contain, they become very brittle when dry. Such as are large and very even are made choice of, and rafped with a knife to remove the outer bark. They are died red by infufing them in the fame dye as is ufed to colour fpunges. When the Roots have remained twenty-four hours in the dye, they are taken out, flowly dried, and varnifhed with two or three coats of a ftrong Mucilage of Gum Tragacanth, each being fuffered to dry before another is laid on. The whole is afterwards repeatedly anointed with Friars Balfam, in order to form a varnifh lefs fufceptible of moifture.

Lucern and Liquerice Roots are dyed and varnifhed in the fame manner : thofe of Marfh-mallows, from the lofs of their Mucilage, confiderably diminifh in thicknefs during the time they ftand in infufion.

47. *Manner of preparing Sponges for the Teeth.*

For this purpofe very thin fponges are made choice of, which are to be wafhed in feveral waters; fqueezing them with the hands, to loofen and force away the little fhells that adhere to their internal furface. Being afterwards dried, they are neatly cut into the fhape of balls about the fize of fmall eggs; and when they have undergone this preparation, they are dyed in the following manner.

Take Brazil Wood rafped, four ounces; Cochineal bruifed, three drachms; Roch Alum, half an ounce; Water, four pints: put them into a proper veflel, and boil till one half of the Liquor is confumed. Then ftrain the decoction through a piece of linen, and pour it hot upon the fponges,

6   which

which are to be left in infufion twelve hours; at the expiration of which time, they are to be repeatedly wafhed in frefh water, as long as any colour proceeds from them. Being dried, they are afterwards dipped in Spirit of Wine, aromatized with Effential Oil of Cinnamon, Cloves, Lavender, &c. The fponges are then fit for ufe, and when dried by fqueezing, are kept in a wide-mouthed glafs-bottle well corked.

48. *Rules for the Prefervation of the Teeth and Gums.*

THE teeth are bones thinly covered with a fine enamel, which is more or lefs ftrong in different perfons. When this enamel is wafted, either by a fcorbutic humour or any external caufe, the tooth cannot long remain found, and muft therefore be cleaned, but with great caution. For this pur-

C 3

pofe

pofe the beft inftrument is a fmall piece of wood, like a butcher's fkewer, rendered foft at the end. It is generally to be ufed alone; only once in a fortnight dip it into a few grains of gunpowder, which has previoufly been bruifed. This will remove every fpot and blemifh, and give your Teeth an inconceivable whitenefs. It is almoft needlefs to fay, that the mouth muft be well wafhed after this operation; for befides the neceffity of fo doing, the faltpetre, &c. ufed in the compofition of Gunpowder, would, if it remained, prove injurious to the gums, &c. but has not, nor can have, any bad effect in fo fhort a time.

It is neceffary to obferve, that very near the gums of people whofe teeth are otherwife good, there is apt to grow a cruft, both within and without, which, if neglected, feparates the gums from the fangs

of

of the teeth; and the latter being by this means left bare, are frequently deſtroyed. This cruſt muſt therefore be carefully ſcraped off.

49. *For ſtopping the Decay of Teeth.*

TAKE of Bole Armenian the quantity of a large nutmeg, a like quantity of Roch Alum, two penny-worth of Cochineal bruiſed, and a ſmall handful of the Chips of Lignum Vitæ; ſimmer them with four ounces of Honey in a new pipkin, for a little time, well ſtirring them all the while, till the ingredients are mixed. In uſing it, take a large ſkewer, on the end of which is tied a piece of linen rag; dip the rag in the medicine, and rub the teeth and gums with it. The longer you abſtain from ſpitting, after the uſe of the remedy, the better. Waſh the mouth well at leaſt once every day, particularly after meals,

firſt

firſt rubbing the teeth with ſalt upon the end of your finger. Teeth much decayed, or uſeleſs, ſhould be drawn, if the operation can be performed with ſafety.

The reader will find ſeveral other receipts for the Teeth, under the article of Waters.

WATERS.

50. *The Celeſtial Water.*

TAKE the beſt Cinnamon, Nutmegs, Ginger, Zedoary, Galangals, and White-Pepper, of each an ounce; ſix Lemon-peels, pared thin; two handfuls of Damaſcene Grapes; as much Jujebs; a handful of Pith of Dwarf-Elder; four handfuls of Juniper-berries perfectly ripe; Fennel-Seeds, Flowers of Sweet Baſil, St. John's-wort, Roſemary, Marjoram, Pennyroyal,

nyroyal, Stechas, Musk Roses, Rue,
Scabious, Centaury, Fumitory, and Agrimony, of each a handful; Spikenard,
Aloes-Wood, Grains of Paradise, Calamus
Aromaticus, Mace, Gum Olibanum, and
Yellow Sanders, of each two ounces;
Hepatic Aloes, fine Amber and Rhubarb,
of each two drachms. All these drugs
being procured good in their kind, beat
in a mortar those that ought to be pulve-
rized, and put the whole, thoroughly mixed
together, into a large strong glass alembic;
pouring as much genuine brandy upon
them as will rise at least three fingers
breadth above the ingredients. Then having well closed the mouth of the alembic,
bury the vessel fifteen days in warm horse-
dung, and afterwards distil the Tincture in
balneo Mariæ, the water almost boiling
hot. When you perceive the water in
the receiver change its colour, instantly

stop

ſtop the proceſs, and ſeparate the phlegm from the ſpirit, by another diſtillation conducted in the ſame manner. The liquor thus obtained is the genuine Celeſtial Water. *Note*, when you perceive this ſecond water begin to loſe its tranſparency, and incline to a reddiſh colour, put it by in a ſtrong glaſs bottle cloſely ſtopped, and diſſolve in the reſidue half a pound of the beſt Treacle, with as much Venice Turpentine and freſh Oil of Almonds. Place the alembic in a ſand heat, and urge the fire to the firſt degree, to have the genuine Balſamic Oil, which ought to be of the conſiſtence of clarified Honey.

If a perſon rubs himſelf in the morning with this water on the forehead, eyelids, back of the head, and nape of the neck, it renders him quick and eaſy of conception, ſtrengthens the memory, enlivens the
ſpirits,

fpirits, and greatly comforts the fight. By putting a few drops with a bit of cotton up the noftrils, it becomes a fovereign cephalic, and cleanfes the brain of all fuperfluous cold and catarrhal humours. If a table fpoonful is drank every third day, it tends to preferve the body in vigour. It is an excellent remedy againft afthmatic complaints, and corrects an offenfive breath.

51. *A Receipt to make the genuine Hungary-Water.*

PUT into an alembic a pound and a half of frefh pickt Rofemary Flowers; Pennyroyal and Marjoram Flowers, of each half a pound; three quarts of good Coniac Brandy; having clofe ftopped the mouth of the alembic to prevent the Spirit from evaporating, bury it twentyeight hours in horfe-dung to digeft, and then diftil off the Spirit in a water-bath.

C 6   A drachm

A drachm of Hungary-Water diluted with Spring-Water, may be taken once or twice a week in the morning fasting. It is also used by way of embrocation to bathe the face and limbs, or any part affected with pains, or debility. This remedy recruits the strength, dispells gloominess, and strengthens the sight. It must always be used cold, whether taken inwardly as a medicine, or applied externally.

52. *Another Receipt to make Hungary-Water.*

FILL a glass or stone cucurbit half full of fresh gathered Rosemary-tops picked in their prime; pour on them as much Spirit of Wine as will thoroughly soak them. Put the vessel in a water-bath, and having closely luted on the head and receiver, leave it to digest on a gentle

fire

fire for three days; at the expiration of which period unlute the veffel, and pour back into the cucurbit whatever liquor you find in the receiver. Then lute your cucurbit again, and encreafe the fire fo as to caufe the Spirit to rife faft over the helm. When about two thirds of the liquor are drawn off, remove the fire, and let the veffel ftand to cool; you will find in the receiver an excellent Hungary-Water, which is to be kept in a glafs bottle clofely ftopped. Hungary-water muft be drawn off with a brifk fire, or the Spirit of Wine will come over the helm, very little impregnated with the effence of Rofemary.

53. *Directions for making Lavender-Water.*

FILL a glafs or earthen body two thirds full of Lavender Flowers, and then fill up the veffel with Brandy or Melaffes Spirits.

Spirits. Let the Flowers ftand in infufion eight days, or lefs if ftraitened for time; then diftil off the Spirit, in a water-bath with a brifk fire, at firft in large drops or even a fmall ftream, that the Effential Oil of the Flowers may rife with the Spirit. But as this cannot be done without the phlegm coming over the helm at the fame time, the Spirit muft be rectified. The firft diftillation being finifhed, unlute the ftill, throw away what remains in the body, and fill it with frefh Flowers of Lavender, in the proportion of two pounds of Lavender Flowers to one pint of Spirit; pour the Spirit already diftilled according to the foregoing directions, on the Lavender Flowers, and diftil a fecond time in a vapour-bath.

54. *Another Method.*

TAKE frefh or dried Lavender Flowers, fprinkle them with White Wine, Brandy, Melaffes

Melaffes Spirit, or Rofe-water; let them
ftand in infufion for fome days, and then
diftil off the Spirit. The diftilled water
will be more odoriferous, if the Flowers
are dried in the fun in a glafs bottle clofe
ftopped, and White Wine afterwards
poured upon them.

If you would have fpeedily, without
the trouble of diftillation, a water impregnated with the flavour of Lavender,
put two or three drops of Oil of Spike,
and a lump of Sugar, into a pint of clear
Water, or Spirit of Wine, and fhake
them well together in a glafs phial, with
a narrow neck. This Water, though
not diftilled, is very fragrant.

55. *To make Rofe-Water.*

To make an excellent Rofe-water,
let the Flowers be gathered two or three
hours

hours after fun-rifing in very fine weather; beat them in a marble mortar into a pafte, and leave them in the mortar foaking in their juice, for five or fix hours; then put the mafs into a coarfe canvas bag, and prefs out the Juice; to every quart of which add a pound of frefh Damafk Rofes, and let them ftand in infufion for twenty-four hours. Then put the whole into a glafs alembic, lute on a head and receiver, and place it on a fand heat. Diftil at firft with a gentle fire, which is to be encreafed gradually till the drops follow each other as quick as poffible; draw off the water as long as it continues to run clear, then put out the fire, and let the alembic ftand till cold. The diftilled water at firft will have very little fragrancy, but after being expofed to the heat of the fun about eight days, in a bottle lightly ftopped with a bit of paper, it acquires an admirable fcent.

56. *Or,*

INFUSE in ten or twenty pints of Juice of Damaſk Roſes, expreſſed in the manner above deſcribed, a proportionable quantity of Damaſk Roſe Leaves gathered with the uſual precautions. After ſtanding in in-fuſion twenty-four hours, pour the whole into a ſhort-necked alembic, diſtil in a ſand heat, and draw off as much as poſſible, taking care not to leave the reſiduum quite dry, for fear the diſtilled water ſhould have an empyreumatic or ſtill-burnt fla-vour. After emptying the alembic, pour the diſtilled water a ſecond time into it, and add a good quantity of freſh picked Damaſk Roſes. Lute it well, placing it again in a ſand heat, and repeat the diſtil-lation. But content yourſelf this time with a little more than half the water you put back into the alembic. To impreſs on Roſe-

water

water the utmoſt degree of fragrancy of which it is ſuſceptible, it is neceſſary to expoſe it to the genial warmth of the ſun.

Roſe-water is an excellent lotion for the eyes, if uſed every morning, and makes a part in all collyriums preſcribed for inflammations of theſe parts; it is alſo proper in many other complaints.

57. To make Orange-Flower Water.

HAVING gathered (two hours before ſun-riſe, in fine weather) a quantity of Orange-Flowers, pluck them leaf by leaf, and throw away the ſtalks and ſtems: fill a tin cucurbit two thirds full of theſe picked Flowers; lute on a low bolt-head, not above two inches higher than the cucurbit; place it in balneo Mariæ, or a water-bath, and diſtill with a ſtrong fire. You run no riſk from preſſing forward the diſtillation

diſtillation with violence, the water-bath effectually preventing the Flowers from being burnt. In this method you pay no regard to the quantity, but the quality of the water drawn off. If nine pounds of Orange Flowers were put into the ſtill, be ſatisfied with three or four quarts of fragrant water; however, you may continue your diſtillation, and ſave even the laſt droppings of the ſtill, which have ſome ſmall fragrancy. During the operation, be careful to change the water in the refrigeratory veſſel as often as it becomes hot. Its being kept cool prevents the diſtilled water from having an empyreumatic or burnt ſmell, and keeps the quinteſſence of the Flowers more intimately united with its phlegm.

58. *Another Method.*

TAKE four pounds of unpicked Orange Flowers, bruiſe them in a marble mortar, and

and pour on them nine quarts of clear Water. Diftil in a cold ftill, and draw off five or fix quarts, which will be exquifitely fragrant. If you are defirous of having it ftill higher flavoured, draw off at firft full feven quarts, unlute the ftill and throw away the refiduum ; empty back the water already diftilled, and add to it two pounds of frefh Orange Flowers bruifed. Again luting the ftill, repeat the diftillation, and draw of five or fix quarts. Then ftop, being careful not to draw off too much water, left the Flowers fhould become dry and burn to.

The ufe of Orange-Flower Water is very extenfive. It is high in efteem for its aromatic perfume; and is ufed with fuccefs for hyfteric complaints.

Waters from all kinds of Flowers are made in the fame manner as Orange-
Flower

Flower and Rofe-water; but waters from dried odoriferous plants, fuch as Thyme, Hyffop, Marjoram and Wormwood, are made as follows.

Fill two thirds of a large ftone jar with the tops of the plant you propofe to diftil; boil, in a fufficient quantity of water, fome twigs or tops of the fame plant; and when one half of the water has evaporated, pour the remainder into a jar over the flowers, and let them ftand to infufe three or four days; then diftil them in a common or cold ftill. Care, however, muft be taken not to diftil to drynefs, left you rifque the bottom of the veffel; to prevent which accident, the beft way is never to draw off more than two thirds of the liquor put into the ftill. If you be defirous that the diftilled water fhould acquire a higher **flavour,** **after** the firft diftillation unlute the ftill,

throw

throw out what remains at the bottom, and fill it half full of fresh tops of the plant, pouring on them the water already diftilled; repeat the diftillation, and this fecond time the water drawn off will be highly odoriferous. If the plant contains a large portion of Effential Oil, it will not fail to float on the top of the liquor contained in the receiver, and may be feparated by the ufual method.

59. *Magifterial Balm-Water.*

TAKE half a pound of Cinnamon, fix ounces of Cardamon-feeds, and the fame quantity of green Anifeeds; Cloves, four ounces; Coriander-feeds, eight ounces: beat thefe fpices in a marble mortar, and putting them afterwards into a ftone jar, add the Yellow Rind of eight Lemons, a pound of Juniper-berries bruifed, twelve handfuls of Balm gathered in its prime,

fix

fix handfuls of Rofemary-tops, as much
Sage, Hyflop, and Angelica, Sweet Marjoram and Thyme, of each fix handfuls;
Wormwood a handful; cut the herbs very
fmall, putting them into the jar with the
fpices, and pour on four gallons of Brandy
or Melaffes Spirits. When they have
flood in infufion eight days, empty the ingredients and liquor into an alembic of a
common height, and diftil in a water-
bath. At firft draw off ten quarts, which
are to be thrown again into the alembic,
continue the fame degree of fire for fome
time, then gradually leffen it till the aromatic fpirit comes off in quick drops. Continue your diftillation in this manner till
you perceived the phlegm rife, which is
eafily known by the weaknefs of the Spirit,
and when the procefs is ended, expofe the
aromatic fpirit which has been drawn off
to the rays of the fun, in a glafs bottle,
stopped

ftopped only with a loofe paper cork, to
give the fiery particles an opportunity of
evaporating. What remains in the body
of the ftill is not to be confidered as wholly
ufelefs. After evaporating it to drynefs,
burn the refiduum of the plants and aromatics; and when the whole mafs is re-
duced to afhes, throw them into a veffel of
boiling water, in which let them remain
two or three minutes on the fire. Then
remove the veffel, and let the water ftand
till cold, when it is to be filtered through
blotting paper. The water, which ap-
pears limpid, is to be fet on the fire again,
and wholly evaporated. At the bottom of
the veffel, which ought to be a new-glazed
earthen pot, will remain a pure white fixed
falt, which may be diffolved in the Ma-
gifterail Balm-water.

This

This water is highly efteemed, and has even acquired a reputation equal to that of Hungary-water, (the receipt for preparing which has been already given) and in particular cafes is preferable.

60. *Compound Balm-Water, commonly called Eau de Carmes.*

TAKE of the frefh Leaves of Balm, a quarter of a pound; Yellow Rind of Lemons, two ounces; Nutmegs and Coriander-feeds, of each one ounce; Cloves, Cinnamon, and Angelica Root, of each half an ounce: having pounded the fpices and feeds, and bruifed the leaves and roots, put them with a quart of Brandy into a glafs cucurbit, of which ftop the mouth, and fet it in a warm place, where let it remain two or three days. Then add a pint of fimple Balm-water, and fhake the whole well together; after

which

which diftil in a vapour bath till the ingredients are left almoft dry ; and preferve
the water thus obtained, in bottles well
ftopped.

This water has been long famous at
Paris and London, and carried thence to
moft parts of Europe. It has the reputation of being a cordial of very extraor-
dinary virtues, and not only of availing
in all lownefs of fpirits, but even in apo-
plexies. It is alfo much efteemed in cafes
of the gont in the ftomach ; whence the
Carmelite Friars, who originally were in
poffeffion of the fecret, have reaped great
benefit from the fale of this water.

61.   *Sweet Honey-Water.*

TAKE of good French Brandy, a gallon;
of the beft Virgin Honey and Coriander-
feeds, each a pound ; Cloves, an ounce
and

and half; Nutmegs, an ounce; Gum Benjamin and Storax, of each an ounce; Vanilloes No. 4; the Yellow Rind of three large Lemons: bruife the Spices and Benjamin, cut the Vanilloes into fmall pieces, put all into a cucurbit, and pour the Brandy on them. After they have digefted forty-eight hours, diftil off the Spirit in a retort with a gentle heat.

To a gallon of this water, add of Damafk Rofe-water and Orange Flower-water, of each a pint and a half; Mufk and Ambergrife, of each five grains; firft grind the Mufk and Ambergrife with fome of the water, and afterwards put all into a large matrafs, fhake them well together, and let them circulate three days and nights in a gentle heat. Then, letting the water cool, filtre and keep it for ufe, in a bottle well ftopped.

It

It is an antiparalytic, fmooths the fkin, and gives one of the moft agrreeable fcents imaginable. Forty or fixty drops put into a pint of clear water, are fufficient to wafh the hands and face.

・

62. *Sweet-fcented Water*.

TAKE Orange Flower-water and Rofe-water, of each an equal quantity; put them into a large wide-mouthed glafs, and ftrew upon the furface gently as much Jafmine Flowers as will cover it; then tie the mouth of the glafs fo carefully that the Flowers be not fhook down to the bot-tom. Repeat the procefs, letting each quantity of the Flowers remain five or fix days, until the water is ftrongly fcented with them. Then diffolve Ambergrife and Mufk, of each a fcruple, in a few ounces of the water, which filtre and put to the reft.

This

This water may also be made by putting the whole into a retort with a sufficient quantity of Jasmine Flowers, and drawing it off in a vapour bath into a receiver well luted.

This is an excellent perfume, and taken inwardly, is of service in some nervous cases and languors.

63. *German sweet-scented Water.*

BEGIN with infusing for eight days in two quarts of Vinegar, two handfuls of Lavender Flowers, as many Provence Roses picked from the stalks, Wild Roses, and Elder Flowers. While they stand in infusion prepare a simple odoriferous water as follows : Put into a glass body the Yellow Rind of three Lemons, sweet Marjoram, Lilies of the Valley and Lavender Flowers, of each two handfuls; pour on them

D 3
a pint

a pint of double diftilled Rofe-water, and
a quart of Spring-water. Lute on a bolt-
head, place the alembic in a fand heat,
fix on a receiver, and leave matters in this
ftate two days, then light a fire under it
and diftil quick. When you have drawn
off a quart, ftop your diftillation, and keep
this fimple odoriferous water for the following ufe.

Take wild Thyme, fweet Marjoram,
fweet Bafil, and Thyme, of each a handful;
Florentine Orrice and Cinnamon, of each
half an ounce; Cloves, Mace, purified
Storax, and Benjamin, of each three
drachms; Labdanum, two drachms; Af-
palathum, half an ounce; Socotrine Aloes,
half a drachm; put all thefe ingredients,
thoroughly bruifed, into a ftone jar, and
add to them the Vinegar infufion, the
diftilled odoriferous water, and a quart
of

of Frontiniac, Mountain, or Cowflip Wine. Stir them well together, and leave the whole to digeft for fifteen days, at the expiration of which time, empty the infufion into a glafs body, large enough to contain a fixth part more liquor; lute on the head, place it in a fand heat, and begin your diftillation with a very gentle fire, increafing it gradually. It fometimes happens that the phlegm of the Vinegar comes over the helm firft; when that is the cafe, fet it afide as ufelefs. As foon as the Spirit begins to rife, which you will directly perceive by its aromatic flavour, fix a receiver on the beak of the alembic, and diftil off about three pints. Keep this by itfelf as the moft fpirituous part of your preparation; and continue to draw off the remainder as long as it runs clear.

D 4 The

The German fweet-fcented Water is penetrating and incifive, admirably revives the vital fpirits, removes head-aches, comforts the heart, is excellent againft unwholefome air, and of courfe a prefervative from contagion.

64. *Imperial Water.*

TAKE five quarts of Brandy, in which diffolve an ounce of Frankincenfe, Maftic, Benjamin, and Gum Arabic; add half an ounce of Cloves and Nutmegs; an ounce and a half of Pine-nut Kernels, and fweet Almonds; with three grains of Mufk. Bruife thefe ingredients in a marble mortar, diftil in a vapour bath, and keep the water that is drawn off in a glafs bottle, clofe ftopped.

This water takes away wrinkles, and renders the fkin extremely delicate; it alfo

whitens

whitens the Teeth, and abates the tooth-ache, fweetens the breath, and ftrengthens the gums. Foreign ladies prize it highly.

65. *Odoriferous Water.*

TAKE fweet Bafil, Mint, fweet Marjoram, Florentine Orrice-root, Hyffop, Balm, Savory, Lavender, and Rofemary, of each a handful; Cloves, Cinnamon, and Nutmegs, of each half an ounce; three or four Lemons, cut in thick flices; infufe them three days in a good quantity of Rofe-water; diftil in a water bath with a gentle fire, and add to the diftilled water a fcruple of Mufk.

66. *Or,*

TAKE fweet Marjoram, Thyme, Lavender, Rofemary, Pennyroyal-buds, red Rofes, Violet-flowers, Clove-july-flowers, Savory, and Orange-peels, of each equal parts; infufe in White Wine till they entirely fink to the bottom of the Wine; then diftil in an alembic, two or three times. Keep the Water in bottles well corked; and preferve the refiduum as a perfume.

67. *The Ladies Water.*

TAKE two handfuls and a half of Red Rofes; Rofemary Flowers, Lavender, and Spikenard, of each a handful; Thyme, Chamomile Flowers, Sage of Virtue, Pennyroyal, and Marjoram, of each a handful; infufe in White Wine twenty-four hours; then put the whole into an alembic; fprinkle it with good White Wine, and throw on it a powder, compofed of an ounce and a half of choice Cloves, Gum Benjamin, and Storax, ftrained, each two drachms. The diftilled Water is to be kept in a bottle well ftopped.

68. *A beautifying Wash.*

TAKE equal parts of White Tanfey, and Rhubarb Water, and to every half pint add two drachms of Sal Ammoniac.

This fluid is applied with a feather or hair pencil, three or four times a day, to pimples or tetters, on any part of the body.

69. *A Cosmetic Water.*

WASH the face with the tears that issue from the Vine, during the months of May and June.

70. *An Excellent Cosmetic.*

PIMPERNEL Water is so sovereign a beautifier of the complexion, that it ought always to have a place on a Lady's toilet.

71. *Venice Water, highly esteemed.*

IN the month of May, take two quarts of Cow's Milk, which pour into a bottle with eight Lemons and four Oranges, sliced; add an ounce of Sugar Candy, and half an ounce of Borax; distil in a water bath or sand heat.

This water is counterfeited at Bagdat in Persia, in the following manner. Take twelve Lemons peeled and sliced, twelve new-laid Eggs, six Sheeps Trotters, four ounces of Sugar Candy, a large slice of Melon, and another of Pompion, with two drachms of Borax; distil in a large glass alembic with a leaden head.

72. *A Balsamic Water.*

TAKE a pound of Venice Turpentine; Oil of Bays, Galbanum, Gum Arabic,

Ivy

Ivy Gum, Frankincenſe, Myrrh, Hepatic Aloes, Aloes-wood, Galangals, Cloves, Comfrey, Cinnamon, Nutmegs, Zedoary, Ginger, and White Dittany, each three ounces; Borax, four ounces; Muſk, a drachm; Ambergriſe, a ſcruple; after bruiſing ſuch of the ingredients as are capable of being powdered, infuſe the whole in ſix quarts of Brandy; and diſtil it. The Balſamic Water drawn off will be good to ſtrengthen the limbs, and cauſe that beauty and vigour which ſo much delights the eye.

73. *Angelic Water, of a moſt agreeable Scent.*

PUT into a large alembic the following ingredients, Benjamin, four ounces; Storax, two ounces; Yellow Sanders, an ounce; Cloves, two drachms; two or three bits of Florentine Orrice, half the Peel of a

Lemon,

Lemon, two Nutmegs, half an ounce of Cinnamon, two quarts of Rofe-water, a pint of Orange Flower-water, and a pint of Magifterial Balm-water. Put the whole into an alembic well luted; diftil in a water bath; and what you draw off will prove an exquifite Angelic Water.

74. *Nofegay or Toilet Water.*

TAKE Honey-water, an ounce; Eau fans Pareille, two ounces; Jafmine-water, not quite five drachms; Clove-water, and Violet-water, of each half an ounce; Cyprus-water, fweet Calamus-water, and Lavender-water, of each two drachms; Spirit of Neroli or Oranges ten drops; mix all thefe Waters together, and keep the mixture in a vial clofe corked.

This water has a delightful fcent; but its ufe is only for the toilet.

75. *Spirit of Guaiacum.*

SPIRIT of Guaiacum is prepared by
infufing two ounces of Guaiacum Shavings in a quart of Brandy, ten or twelve
days, fhaking the veffel now and then.
The Tincture is then filtred through paper,
and ufed to gargle the mouth in the fame
manner as the Vulnerary-water.

76.   *The Divine Cordial.*

To make this, take, in the beginning
of the month of March, two ounces of
the Roots of the true Acorus, Betony,
Florentine Orrice-roots, Cyprus, Gentian,
and fweet Scabious; an ounce of Cinnamon, and as much Yellow Sanders; two
drachms of Mace; an ounce of Juniper-
berries; and fix drachms of Coriander-
feeds; beat thefe ingredients, in a mortar,
to a coarfe powder, and add thereto the

7   outer

outer Peel of fix fine China Oranges; put them all into a large veffel, with a gallon and a half of Spirit of Wine; fhake them well, and then cork the veffel tight till the feafon for Flowers. When thefe are in full viguor, add half a handful of the following: viz. Violets, Hyacinths, Jonquils, Wall Flowers, Red, Damafk, White, and Mufk Rofes, Clove-july-flowers, Orange Flowers, Jafmine, Tuberofes, Rofemary, Sage, Thyme, Lavender, fweet Marjoram, Broom, Elder, St. John's-wort, Marigold, Chamomile, Lilies of the Valley, Narciffufes, Honeyfuckle, Borage, and Buglofs.

Three feafons are required to procure all thefe Flowers in perfection; Spring, Summer, and Autumn. Every time you gather any of thefe Flowers, add them immediately to the infufion, mixing them

thoroughly

thoroughly with the other ingredients; and three days after you have put in the laſt Flowers, put the whole into a glaſs cucurbit, lute on the head carefully, place it in a water bath over a flow fire, keep the receiver cool, and draw off five quarts of Spirit, which will prove of a rare quality. As a medicine, it is far more efficacious than Balm-water; and for its fine ſcent, one of the beſt perfumes.

77. *Compound Cyprus Water.*

TAKE a gallon of Spirit of Jaſmine, infuſe in it half an ounce of Florentine Orrice groſsly powdered, a quarter of an ounce of bruiſed Angelica-ſeeds, three ſcraped Nutmegs, three ounces of White Muſk-roſes bruiſed, a drachm of Spirit of Orange, and fifteen drops of Eſſence of Ambergriſe. If it is not the ſeaſon for Roſes, when you make this Water,

put

put inftead of them a pint of Rofe-water feented with Mufk, and if that cannot be procured, ufe common Rofe-water; draw off the Spirit in a water bath, and in a ftream like a thread; taking care to place the receiver in cold water, that the Spirit may cool as faft as poffible and thereby the better preferve its perfume.

78. *Imperial Water.*

PUT into a gallon of Brandy, a quarter of a pound of picked Violets, an ounce of Florentine Orrice, a quarter of a pound of Double Jonquils, two ounces of picked Orange Flowers, two Ounces of White Mufk-rofes, three ounces of Tuberofes, a drachm of Mace, half a drachm of Cloves, an ounce of Quinteffence of Bergamot, and an ounce of Quinteffence of Oranges. All the Flowers muft be gathered in their proper feafon. Obferve to put

into

into the Brandy at the same time with the Violets, the Orrice, Mace, and Cloves, in grofs powder, then add the different Flowers as they come in feafon, remembering not to add the quinteffences, till after the Tuberofes, which are the laft Flower. Every time you put in a frefh Flower, fhake the veffel, and cork it very tight. Eight days after the Tuberofes have been infufed, put the whole into a glafs body, lute on the head carefully, and place under the receiver an earthen veffel filled with cold water, that the Spirit may cool as faft as it comes over, by which means its fcent will be the better preferved. You may draw off two quarts of a rectified Spirit, that will give perfect fatisfaction to the moft delicate judge.

79. *All Flower Water.*

POUR into a large veffel five quarts of strong Spirit of Wine, and infufe in it the following Flowers, as they come in feafon: Violets, Hyacinths, and Wall Flowers, of each a quarter of a pound; fingle and double Jonquils, of each two ounces; a quarter of a pound of Lilies of the Valley, and the fame quantity of Spanifh Jafmine; half an ounce of Rofemary Flowers; an ounce of Elder Flowers; two ounces of Wild, Damafk, and White Rofes, bruifed; three ounces of Orange Flowers; a quarter of a pound of Clove-july-flowers, Syringo Bloffoms, Tuberofes, and Tops of Mint in Flower; and thirty drops of Quinteffence of Mufk-feed. The latter, however, need not be added till the time of diftillation, which muft not be till three days after the laft Flowers have been infufed.

fufed. Perform the operation in a water bath, and having carefully luted the head and receiver, which muſt be placed in a tub of cold water, to preſerve the ſcent, draw off about three quarts and a pint with a moderate fire, then change the receiver, fix on another, and draw off another pint, which, though of an inferior quality, is well worth preſerving.

80. *A curious Water, known by the Name of the Spring Noſegay.*

TAKE fix ounces of Hyacinths, a quarter of a pound of picked Vio ets, the ſame quantity of Wall Flowers picked, and Jonquils; an ounce of Florentine Orrice bruiſed; half an ounce of Mace grofsly powdered; and two ounces of Quinteſfenſe of Orange. Put the whole (the Jonquils, Wall Flowers, and Lilies of the Valley excepted) about the end of

6   March,

March, into a glafs body, with a gallon
of ftrong Spirit of Wine; bruife the
Hyacinths, Violets, Orrice, and Mace;
and towards the end of April, add the
Jonquils, when in their perfection, that
is to fay, when full blown. A few days
after, put in the Wall Flowers, the
Petals only; then add the Lilies of the
Valley, carefully picked, and fhake all the
ingredients well : Eight days after having
put in this laft Flower, empty the infufion into an alembic, lute on a head
and receiver, which muft be placed in
cold water, and diftil in a water bath,
with a gentle fire. From the above quantity three quarts of excellent Spirit may
be drawn off, that juftly deferves the ap-
pellation of the Spring Nofegay.

81. *A Cosmetic Water, of great Use to prevent Pits after the Small-Pox.*

DISSOLVE an ounce and a half of Salt in a pint of Mint-water; boil them together, and skim the Liquor. This is a very useful Wash for the face after the Small-Pox, in order to clear away the scabs, allay the itching, and remove the redness.

82. *A Cooling Wash.*

INFUSE in a sufficient quantity of clear Water, some Bran, Yolks of Eggs, and a grain or two of Ambergrise, for three or four hours; then distil the Water, which will prove an excellent Cosmetic, and clear the skin supprisingly. It is of service to keep it in the sun eight or ten days, in a bottle well corked.

The distilled Waters of Melons, Bean Flowers, the Wild-Vine, green or unripe Barley,

Barley, and the Water that is found in vesicles on the leaves of the elm-tree, may also be used for the same intention.

83. *An excellent Water to clear the Skin, and take away Pimples.*

TAKE two quarts of Water, in which a quantity of Horse-beans has been boiled till quite soft; put it into an alembic, and add two handfuls of Pin pernel, the same quantity of White Tansy, a pound of Veal minced small, six new-laid Eggs, and a pint of White-Wine Vinegar; distil this mixture in a water-bath, and it will afford an excellent Lotion to remove all eruptions on the face, if washed with it every night and morning.

84. *Another.*

KNEAD a Loaf with three pounds of Wheaten Flour, a pound of Bean Flour, and

and Goats Milk, with Mild Yeaſt or Leaven. Bake it in an oven, ſcoop out the crumb, and ſoak it thoroughly in new Goats Milk and ſix Whites of Eggs; add an ounce of calcined Egg-ſhells. Mix all well together, and diſtil in a ſand heat. You will obtain an excellent coſmetic water, by waſhing with which every day, the face will become ſmooth and clear.

85. *Venetian Water to clear a Sun-burnt Complexion.*

TAKE a pint of Cow's Milk, or, in the month of May, a pint of the Water that diſtils from the Vine when wounded, eight Lemons and four Seville Oranges cut in thin ſlices, two ounces of Sugar Candy, half an ounce of Borax in fine powder, and four Narciſſus Roots beaten to a paſte; diſtil theſe ingredients in a

E　　　　vapour-

vapour-bath. Rectify the distilled Liquor by the same method, and keep it in a bottle closely corked.

86. *A Water for Pimples in the Face.*

BOIL together a handful of the herbs Patience, and Pimpernel in Water; and wash yourself every day with the decoction.

87. *A Fluid to clear a tanned Skin.*

TAKE unripe Grapes, soak them in Water, sprinkle them with Alum and Salt, then wrap them up in paper, and roast them in hot ashes; squeeze out the Juice, and wash the face with it every morning, it will soon remove the Tan.

88. *A Fluid to whiten the Skin.*

TAKE equal parts of the Roots of Centaury and the White Vine, a pint of

Cow's

Cow's Milk, and the crumb of a Wheaten Loaf; diftil in a glafs alembic. The diftilled Water, for ufe, muft be mixed with an equal quantity of Hungary Water: it then admirably clears the complexion.

The diftilled Waters of Fennel, and White Lilies, with a little Gum Maftic, will produce the fame effect.

89. *A Beautifying Wafh.*

PUT into a cucurbit five pints of French Brandy; add to it a pound and a half of Crumb of Bread, three ounces of Plum-tree-gum, two ounces of Litharge of Silver in fine powder, and four ounces of fweet Almonds. The ingredients are to be beat together into a pafte, and left to digeft in the Spirit eight days; then diftil in a vapour-bath, and wafh the face and

hands

hands with the water thus obtained. It muſt be ſuffered to dry on the ſkin without being wiped off, and the complexion will preſently become clear and gloſſy.

90. *A diſtilled Water that tinges the Cheeks a beautiful Carnation* **Hue.**

TAKE two quarts of White Wine Vinegar, three ounces of Iſinglaſs, two ounces of bruiſed Nutmegs, and ſix ounces of Honey; diſtil with a gentle fire, and add to the diſtilled Water a ſmall quantity of Red Sanders, in order to colour it. Before the Tincture is uſed, a Lady ſhould waſh herſelf with Elder-flower Water, and then the cheeks will become of a fine lively vermillion, that cannot be diſtinguiſhed from the natural bloom of youth.

91. *A Cosmetic Water.*

TAKE three Aron Roots minced small, three Melons of a middling size, three Cucumbers, four new laid Eggs, a slice of a Pumkin, two Lemons, a pint of Whey, a gallon of Rose-water, a quart of Water-lily-water, a pint of Plantain, as much White Tansy-water, and half an ounce of Borax. Distil the whole together in a vapour-bath.

92. *A Water, christened, the Fountain of Youth.*

TAKE an ounce of Sulphur Vivum; Olibanum and Myrrh, each two ounces; six drachms of Amber; a quart of Rose-water; distil the whole in a vapour-bath, and wash yourself with the Water every night going to rest: the next morning wash yourself with weak Barley-water,

and

and your complexion will have a youthful air.

It is afferted alfo that the diftilled Water of green Pine-apples takes away wrinkles, and gives the complexion an air of youth.

93. *A Water to preferve the Complexion.*

Mix together Water-lily Water, Bean-flower Water, Melon Water, Cucumber Water, and Lemon Juice, of each an ounce; to which add, of Bryony, Wild Succory, White Lilies, Borrage and Bean Flowers, each a handful. Take feven or eight White Pigeons, pick them, and cut off their heads and pinions, mince the reft of them fmall, and put them into an alembic with the other ingredients. To thefe add four ounces of Sugar Candy in powder, as much Camphor, and the Crumb of three fmall Wheaten Loaves, each weigh-

weighing about half a pound; digeſt the whole eighteen or twenty days in an alembic, then diſtil, and keep the Water that is drawn off in proper veſſels for uſe. Before waſhing with it, carefully obſerve to cleanſe the face with the following compoſition.

Take a quarter of a pound of the Crumb of Rye Bread hot from the oven, the Whites of four new laid Eggs, and a pint of White Wine Vinegar; beat the whole well together, and ſtrain through a linen rag. The uſe of theſe two preparations perfectly cleanſes and clears the ſkin, preſerves its freſhneſs, and prevents wrinkles.

E 4

94. *A Water that gives a Gloſs to the Skin.*

Take a handful of Bean, Elder, and Bugloſs Flowers, a ſmall Pigeon clean drawn, the Juice of two Lemons, four ounces of Salt, and five ounces of Camphor; diſtil them in a vapour-bath; add to the diſtilled Water a few grains of Muſk, and expoſe it to the ſun for the ſpace of a month, obſerving to take the veſſel within doors every night. The way to uſe this Water, is to dip the corner of a fine napkin in it, and gently rub the face.

95. *A Preſervative from Tanning.*

Infuse in clean Water for three days a pound of Lupines, then take them out, and boil them in a copper veſſel with five quarts of freſh Water. When the Lu-

pines

pines are boiled tender, and the Water grows rather ropy, prefs out the Liquor, and keep it for ufe. Whenever you are under a neceffity of expofing yourfelf to the fun, wafh the face and neck with this preparation.

The Oil of unripe Olives, in which a fmall quantity of Gum Maftic has been diffolved, poffeffes the fame virtue.

96. To remove Freckles.

TAKE Houfeleek, and Celandine, of each an equal quantity; diftil in a fand heat, and wafh with the diftilled Water.

97. Or,

APPLY the Juice of Onions to the part affected.

E 5

98. *Or,*

BOIL Ivy Leaves in Wine, and foment the face with the decoction.

99. *A Water to prevent Freckles, or Blotches in the Face.*

TAKE Wild Cucumber-roots and Narciffus-roots, of each an equal quantity; dry them in the fhade, and reduce them to a very fine powder, putting them afterwards into ftrong French Brandy, with which wafh the face, till it begins to itch; and then wafh it with cold water. This method muft be repeated every day till a perfect cure is obtained, which will foon happen, for this water has a flight cauftic property, and of courfe muft remove all fpots on the fkin.

100. *Or,*

TAKE a handful of fresh Wood-ashes, boil them in a pint of clear Water, till one half is wasted away, then pour off the Liquor as long as it runs clear ; boil it again a little while, and filter it through coarse paper.

101. *A Water to improve the Complexion.*

TAKE Snakeweed-roots and Narcissus-roots, of each an equal quantity ; a pint of Cow's Milk, and the Crumb of a Wheaten Loaf; distil these ingredients in a glass alembic. This Water should be mixed with an equal quantity of Hungary-water.

102. *Or,*

TAKE Chich Peas, French Beans, and Garden Beans, of each four ounces; peel off their skins, powder them, and infuse

E 6

in

in a quart of White Wine; add the Gall of an Ox, and the Whites of fifteen new laid Eggs. Mix the ingredients thoroughly, diſtil in a glaſs alembic with a ſand heat; and waſh the face with the diſtilled Water, as occaſion requires.

103. *A Coſmetic Water.*

TAKE a pound and a half of fine Wheaten Bread, four ounces of Peach Kernels, the ſame quantity of the four Cold Seeds, viz. Gourd-ſeed, Cucumber-ſeed, Melon-ſeed, and Lettuce-ſeed; the Whites of twelve new laid Eggs, the Juice of four Lemons, three ounces of Sugar Candy, a gallon of Goat's Milk; mix the whole together, and diſtil in a vapour-bath. To every two quarts of the diſtilled Water, add a quarter of a pint of Spirit of Cherries.

104. *Or,*

TAKE fix Aron Roots minced fmall, fix ounces of Bran, four ounces and a half of Myrrh in powder, three pints of Milk, and the fame quantity of Wine; diftil according to the rules of art; and to the diftilled Water add a fmall bit of Alum.

105. *A fimple Balfamic Water, which re-moves Wrinkles.*

TAKE Barley-water, ftrained through a piece of fine linen cloth, and drop into it a few drops of Balm of Gilead; fhake the bottle for feveral hours, until the Balfam is entirely incorporated with the Water, which is known by the turbid milky appearance of the Mixture. This greatly improves the complexion, and preferves the bloom of youth. If ufed only once

a day,

a day, it takes away wrinkles, and gives the ſkin a ſurpriſing luſtre. Before this fluid is uſed, the face ſhould be waſhed clean with rain water.

106. *A Water to change the Eyebrows black.*

FIRST waſh your eyebrows with a de-coction of Gall Nuts ; then wet them with a pencil or little bruſh dipped in a ſolution of Green Vitriol, in which a little Gum Arabic has been diſſolved, and when dry, they will appear of a beautiful black colour.

107. *To remove Worms in the Face.*

MAKE uſe of the diſtilled Waters of the Whites of Eggs, Bean Flowers, Water Lilies, White Lilies, Melon Seeds, Iris Roots, Solomon's Seal, White Roſes, or crumb of Wheaten Bread, either mixed together,

together, or feparately, with the addition
of the White of a new-laid Egg.

108. *The Duchefs de la Vrilliere's Mouth-Water.*

TAKE Cinnamon, two ounces; Cloves,
fix drachms; Water Creffes, fix ounces;
frefh Lemon Peel, an ounce and a half;
Red Rofe Leaves, an ounce; Scurvy Grafs,
half a pound; Spirit of Wine, three pints.
Bruife the Spices, cut the Water Creffes
and Scurvy Grafs fmall, and macerate the
whole in Spirit of Wine, in a bottle well
corked, during twenty-four hours; then
diftil to drynefs in a vapour-bath, and afterwards rectify the diftilled Water, by
repeating the fame procefs.

This Water ftrengthens the gums, prevents the fcurvy, and cures aphthæ, or
little ulcerations in the mouth. It is
ufed

ufed to gargle the mouth with, either by itfelf, or diluted with water, as occafion. may require.

109. *Another Water for the Teeth, called Spirituous Vulnerary Water.*

FOR this intention are commonly ufed Spirituous Waters, that are no ways difagreeable; waters proper to ftrengthen and fortify the gums, as Spirituous Vulnerary Water tinctured with Cochineal, or Seed Lac; Guaiacum Water, or the Duchefs de la Vrilliere's Water above defcribed.

To tinge Vulnerary Water, put any quantity into a glafs matrafs, and infufe in it fome bruifed Cochineal; then filter the Vulnerary Water, and ufe it to gargle the mouth, after which the teeth are to be cleaned with Tooth Powder. This, when

found

found too ftrong, may be lowered by the addition of Spring Water.

110. *Receipt to make Vulnerary Water.*

TAKE frefh gathered Leaves of Sage, Angelica, Wormwood, Savory, Fennel, and fpiked Mint, of each four ounces; Leaves of Hyffop, Balm, Sweet Bafil, Rue, Thyme, Marjoram, Rofemary, Origanum, Calamint, and Wild Thyme, frefh gathered, of each four ounces; the fame quantity of Lavender Flowers, and a gallon of rectified Spirit of Wine.

CUT the Herbs fmall, infufe them teh or twelve hours in Spirit of Wine, and then diftil in a vapour-bath. Preferve the Spirit drawn off, in a bottle well corked.

111. *A Water for the Gums.*

TAKE of the beſt Cinnamon, an ounce ; Cloves, three drachms ; the Yellow Peel of two Lemons ; Red Roſe Leaves, half an ounce ; Water Creſſes, half a pound ; Scurvy Graſs, four ounces ; rectified Spirit of Wine, three gallons : bruiſe the Spices, and infuſe the whole a ſufficient time in the Spirit in a glaſs veſſel ; then diſtil off the Spirit for uſe, in a vapour-bath.

112. *Another, prepared by Infuſion.*

TAKE two drachms of Cinnamon, finely powdered ; half a drachm of Cloves, in fine powder ; and half an ounce of Roch Alum : pour on them three gallons of boiling Water ; when cold, add ſix ounces of Plantain Water, half an ounce of Orange-flower Water, a quarter of an ounce of Eſſence of Lemons, and a gill and a half of
rectified

rectified Spirit of Wine; let the whole stand together in digestion four and twenty hours, then filter through paper, and reserve the clear water for use.

113. *Or*,.

TAKE Mace, Cinnamon, Cloves, Pellitory of Spain, and Terra Sigillata, or Sealed Earth, of each half an ounce; beat the whole together in a mortar, and infuse it a month in a quart of Spirit of Wine. Strain off the Spirit, and add eight ounces of Spirit of Scurvy Grafs. Drop six or feven drops in a glafs of very clear Water, and rince the mouth; afterwards rubbing the gums with conferve of Hips acidulated with five or six drops of Spirit of Vitriol.

114. *Another Water for the Gums.*

TAKE of the beſt Cinnamon, an ounce; Cloves, three drachms; the Peel of two Lemons; half an ounce of Red Roſe Leaves; half a pound of Water Creſſes, four ounces of Scurvy Graſs, and three gallons of rectified Spirit of Wine. Bruiſe the Spices, and let the whole ſtand in digeſtion in a glaſs veſſel twenty-four hours; then diſtil in a vapour-bath.

115. *A ſimple Depilatory.*

OIL of Walnuts frequently rubbed on a child's forehead, will prevent the hair from growing on that part.

116. *Prepared Sponges for the Face.*

STEEP in Water ſome time the fineſt and thinneſt Sponges you can pick out; waſh them well, dry them, and ſoak them

in

in Brandy a whole day; then fqueeze the Brandy out, and dry them again. Laftly, dip them in Orange-flower Water, and let them remain in it eleven or twelve hours. When fqueezed, and thoroughly dried, they are fit for ufe.

117. *Spirit of Rofes.*

To make the inflammable Spirit of Rofes, take twenty pounds of Damafk Rofes, beat them to a Pafte, in a marble mortar; put this Pafte, layer by layer, with fea falt, into a large ftone jar, or two jars, if one is not large enough to contain the whole quantity; that is to fay, fprinkle every layer of the Pafte about half an inch thick with Salt; and prefs the layers of Rofes as clofe together as poffible. Cork the jar with a waxed cork, cover the upper-moft end of the cork, and the edges of the mouth of the jar, with wax alfo, and place

place it fix weeks, or two months, in a vault, or fome other cool place. At the expiration of this period, open the jar; if it exhales a ftrong vinous fmell, the fermentation has arrived at its proper height; but if you do not perceive fuch an odour, throw into the jar a little Yeaft, and ftop it clofe in the fame manner as before. A ftrong fermentation having been excited, take five or fix pounds of your fermented Rofe Pafte, put it into a common cucurbit, and diftil it with a very gentle fire in a vapour-bath. When you have drawn off as much water as you can, unlute the alembic; throw away what remains in the cucurbit, take five or fix pounds more of the fermented Pafte of Rofes, and put it into the cucurbit, with the Water already drawn; diftil in a vapour-bath with fuch a degree of fire, as will caufe the diftilled Water

to

to run off in a middling fized ftream. When you can draw off no more, empty the cucurbit, fill it again with freſh fermented Paſte of Roſes, and pour on it all the diſtilled Water that the preceding diſtillations have produced. Diſtil as before; and repeat theſe operations, till you have uſed all your fermented Paſte of Roſes. Every time you open the jar, be careful to cork it cloſe, otherwiſe the moſt ſpirituous particles will evaporate. After the laſt diſtillation, you will have obtained a very fine ſcented Water, but not very ſpirituous, becauſe loaded with a conſiderable quantity of phlegm; and it muſt therefore be rectified.

For this purpoſe make choice of a very long necked glaſs matraſs of a reaſonable ſize, fill it about three parts full with your unrectified Spirit of Roſes; fit on a bolt-

head,

I

head, and receiver; lute the joints carefully, and diftil in a vapour-bath with a very flow fire. When you have drawn off about a tenth part of what was put into the matrafs, let the veffel cool, and fct apart the Spirit that is found in the re-ceiver. What remains in the matrafs muft not be thrown away as ufelefs, for it is a Rofe-water far fuperior to what is pre-pared according to the ufual method.

After the firft rectification of a part of the Spirit, repeat the fame operation with another part, till the whole is rectified, and then rectify them all together once more. After this laft operation, you will obtain a highly penetrating and inflam-mable Spirit of Rofes. The phlegmatic part that remains in the matrafs may be added to that procured from the preceding rectifications, and the whole kept for ufe

in

in a cellar or other cool place in a bottle, well corked.

The scent of inflammable Spirit of Roses is extremely sweet; if only two drops of it are mixed with a glass of Water, they impart to the Water so high a perfume, that it exceeds the very best Rose-water.

118. *Inflammable Spirits of all Kinds of Flowers.*

To distil an inflammable Spirit from Flowers of all kinds, the preceding method must be used; as also to procure one from all kinds of vegetables. Only observe that in plants, and dried flowers, as Thyme, Betony, Mint, Stechas, Violets, and Jasmine, the Seeds must be bruised with the Flowers and Roots; as

F they

they alfo muft with the Flowers of the
Tuberofe Lily, Angelica, Iris, in odoriferous Fruits, as Oranges, Lemons,
Citrons, &c. add the Rind of thofe
Fruits to the Flowers; and to the Flowers
of Elder, Juniper, Lily of the Valley,
and Acacia, &c. add the Berries well
moiftened; whether green or dry is of
no fignification.

ESSENCES.

119. *Method of extracting Effences from
Flowers.*

Procure a wooden box lined with tin,
that the wood may not communicate any
difagreeable flavour to the Flowers, nor
imbibe the Effence. Make feveral ftraining frames to fit the Box, each about two
inches thick, and drive in them a number
of hooks, on which fix a piece of cal-
licoe

licoe ftretched tight. The utmoft care is requifite, to have the ftraining cloths perfectly clean and dry before they are ufed.

After having caufed the cloths to imbibe as much Oil of Ben as poffible, fqueeze them a little, then ftretch and fix them on the hooks of the frames; put one frame thus completed at the bottom of the box, and upon its cloth ftrow equally thofe flowers, the effence of which you intend to extract; cover them with another frame, on the cloth of which you are to ftrow more flowers, and continue to act in the fame manner till the box is quite filled. The frames being each about two inches thick, the flowers undergo very little preffure, though they lye between the cloths. At the expiration of twelve hours, apply frefh flowers in

F 2

the

the fame manner, and continue fo to do for fome days. When you think the fcent powerful enough, take the cloths from the frames, fold them in four, roll them up, and tie them tight with a piece of whip-cord, to prevent their ftretching out too much, then put them into a prefs, and fqueefe out the oil. The prefs muft be lined with tin, that the wood may not imbibe any part of the oil. Place underneath a very clean earthen or glafs veffel to receive the effence, which is to be kept in bottles nicely corked.

The effence of one kind of flower only, can be made in a box at the fame time, for the fcent of one would impair that of another. For the fame reafon, the cloths that have been ufed to extract the effence of any particular flower, cannot be ufed to extract the effence of another, till
washed

wafhed clean in a ftrong lye, and thoroughly dried in the open air. This method is of great ufe to obtain the fcent of
flowers whhich afford no Effential Oil by
diftillation, fuch as Tuberofes, Jafmine,
and feveral others.

120. *Or,*

TAKE any flowers you pleafe, and put
them in a large jar, layer by layer, mixed
with Salt, as directed for inflammable
Spirit of Rofes, till the jar is quite full;
then cork it tight, and let it ftand in a
cellar. or fome other cool place, for forty
days; at the expiration of which time,
empty the whole into a fieve, or ftraining
cloth, ftretched over the mouth of a glazed
earthen or ftone pan, to receive the effence
that drains from the flowers upon fqueezing them gently. Afterwards put the
effence into a glafs bottle, which muft not

F 3   be

be filled above two thirds; cork it tight, and expofe it to the heat of the fun in fine weather, five and twenty or thirty days, to purify the effence, a fingle drop of which will be capable of fcenting a quart of Water or any other Liquid.

121. *Effence of Ambergrife.*

TAKE of Ambergrife a quarter of an ounce; the fame quantity of Sugar Candy; Mufk, half a drachm; and Civet, two grains; rub them together, and put the mixture into a Phial: pour upon it a quarter of a pint of tartarifed Spirit of Wine, ftop clofe the Phial, which fet in a gentle fand heat for four or five days, and then decant the clear Tincture for ufe. This makes the beft of perfumes; the leaft touch of it leaves its fcent upon any thing a great time; and in con-
ftitutions

ftitutions where such sweets are not offenfive to the head, nothing can be a more
immediate Cordial.

122. *A Remedy for St. Anthony's Fire or
Eryfipelatous Eruptions on the Face.*

TAKE Narciffus Roots, an ounce; fresh
Nettle-feeds, half an ounce; beat them
together into a foft Pafte with a fufficient
quantity of White Wine Vinegar, and
anoint the eruptions therewith every night;
or, bathe the part affected with the Juice
of Creffes.

FLOWERS.

123. *Manner of drying Flowers, fo as to preferve their natural Colours.*

TAKE fine White Sand, wafh it repeatedly, till it contains not the leaft earth

F 4   or

or falt, then dry it for ufe. When thoroughly dry, fill a glafs or ftone jar half full of Sand, in which ftick the Flowers in their natural fituation, and afterwards cover them gently with the fame, about the eighth part of an inch above the Flower. Place the glafs in the fun, or, if in winter-time, in a room where a conftant fire is kept, till the Flower is perfectly dried. Then remove the Sand with the utmoft precaution, and clean the Leaves with a feather brufh. Particular Flowers lofe in fome meafure their natural lively colours, but this may be helped by the afliftance of art.

Rofes and other Flowers of a delicate colour, recover their natural luftre by being expofed to a moderate vapour of Brimftone; but Crimfon or Scarlet Flowers, by being expofed to the vapour

of

of a folution of Tin in Spirit of Nitre. The vapour of a folution of Filings of Steel in Spirit of Vitriol, reftores to the Leaves and Stalk, their primitive green colour. This method fucceeds perfectly well in fingle Flowers. There are fome difficulties with refpect to Pinks, Carnations, and other double Flowers; to fucceed with them, fplit the cup on each fide, and when the Flower is quite dry, glue it together with Gum-water; or prick the cup in different parts with a large pin.

As to the fcent, which is in great meafure loft in drying, it may be reftored, by dropping into the middle of the Flower a drop of its Effential Oil; for inftance, a drop of Oil of Rofes on a Rofe, Oil of Cloves on a Clove-july-flower, Oil of Jafmine on a Jafmine Flower.

F 5

124. *A Secret to preserve Flowers.*

FILL an earthen, copper, or wooden veffel half full of fifted Sand, then fill it up to the brim with clear Spring Water, and ftir the Sand well with a ftick in order to detach the earthy particles. When the Sand has thoroughly fettled, pour off the turbid Water by incli- nation, add frefh Water, and continue to wafh the Sand, till all the Water that floats on its furface remains perfectly clear. The Sand being thus cleanfed, expofe it to the heat of the fun a fufficient time, to exhale entirely its humidity. Prepare for every Flower an earthen or tin veffel of a proper fize, make choice of the fineft, moft perfect, and drieft Flowers of their refpective kinds, and be careful to leave the ftalks of a good length. Place

them,

them upright in the veffel, with one hand as lightly as poffible, about two or three inches below the rims, fo as not to touch the fides, or each other; and with the other hand gradually pour on them the Sand till the ftalk is quite covered; then lightly cover the Flower itfelf, feparating the Leaves a little. The Tulip requires a farther operation. The triangular top that rifes out of the middle of the cup, muft be cut off, by which means the Leaves of the Flower will adhere better to the Stalk. When the veffel is filled with Flowers, leave it a month or two expofed to the rays of the fun; and the Flowers when taken out, though dry, will be very little inferior in beauty to new-blown Flowers, but will have loft their fcent.

F 6

TAKE the fineſt River Sand you can get, after having ſifted it ſeveral times through a fine ſieve, throw it into a glaſs veſſel full of clear Water, and rub it a good while between your fingers to render it ſtill finer; then pour off the Water by inclination, and dry the Sand in the ſun. The Sand being thus pre-pared, bury the Flowers gently in it with their Leaves and Stalk, diſpoſing them in ſuch a manner that their form may not be in the leaſt injured. After hav-ing thus kept Flowers ſome time, till their humid particles are entirely evapo-rated, take them out, and incloſe them in bottles, well corked; ſecure them from all changes of the atmoſphere, but let them enjoy a temperate warmth; for if the heat is too great, the colours fade;

and

and if not kept fufficiently warm, the humidity of the Flowers will not wholly evaporate.

126. *Another Method of preferving Flowers
a long while, in their natural Shape and
Colour.*

TAKE the fineft River Sand, divefted of
whatever impurities it may contain; then
dry it in the fun or a ftove, fift it through
a fieve, and only make ufe of the fineft
part. Procure a Tin Box, or a Wooden
Box lined with Tin, of any fize you
think proper, cover the bottom of the
Box three or four inches deep with prepared Sand, and ftick in it the Stalks
of the Flowers in rows, but in fuch a
manner that none of the Flowers may
touch each other, afterwards filling the
vacuities between the Stalks with Sand.
Then fpread the Sand all round the Flowers,

which

which cover with a layer about two or three inches thick. Put this Box in a place expofed to the fun, or in fome warm fituation, for the fpace of a month. With refpect to Tulips, the piftil that rifes in the middle, and contains the Seed, muft be dexteroufly cut out, and the empty fpace filled with Sand: too many Flowers fhould not be put into the fame Box, nor fhould the Box be too large.

GLOVES.

127. *White Gloves fcented With Jafmine after the Italian manner.*

TAKE half an ounce of White Wax, diffolve it over a gentle fire in two ounces of Oil of Ben. Drefs your fkins with this Liquid, dry them on lines, and clean

them

them well with the pureſt water; when they are dried and properly ſtretched, make them up into gloves, which are to have the Jaſmine Flowers applied to them eight days according to the uſual method; then bring them into ſhape, and fold them ſmooth. This manner of working them up, communicates to the gloves the property of retaining the ſcent of the Flowers much better than thoſe that are dreſt otherwiſe, and likewiſe imparts to them the virtue of preſerving the hands and arms delicately ſoft and white.

128. *Gloves ſcented without Flowers.*

TAKE an ounce of Liquid Storax, an ounce of Roſe-wood, the ſame quantity of Florentine Orrice, and half an ounce of Yellow Sanders. Beat the three laſt articles into a very fine powder, and add to it the Storax, with the earths that

you

you ufe to dye your gloves, and a little
Gum Arabic. Then take an equal
quantity of Rofe and Orange Flower
Water, to temper this compofition which
you lay on your gloves; when they are
dry, rub them well, and fold them up;
then drefs them afrefh with a little Gum
Water, in which has been diffolved fome
powder of Florentine Orrice; hang them
up to dry, and afterwards bring them into
form, and fold them up as fit for ufe.

129. *White Gloves fcented with Ketmia or
Mufk Seed.*

TAKE an ounce of Yellow Sanders,
an ounce of Florentine Orrice, an ounce
of Gum Benjamin, two ounces of Rofe-
wood, and a drachm of Storax; reduce the
whole to fine powder, with as much
Cerufs as you choofe. Mix them with
Rofe-water, and drefs your gloves with
the

the mixture as neatly as you can for
the firſt coat; then rub them well, and
open them when they are thoroughly dry.
Uſe the ſame for the ſecond coat, with the
addition of a little Gum Arabic. For
the third coat, levigate on a marble, eight
grains of Ketmia Seed, four grains of
Civet, a little Oil of Ben, and a very
little Gum Tragacanth, diſſolved in Roſe-
water; add to this compoſition a quarter
of a pint of Orange Flower Water; after
having applied this third coat to your
gloves, bring them into form, before they
get thoroughly dry.

130. *To colour Gloves a curious French Yellow.*

TAKE Chalk and Wood Aſhes, of each
an equal quantity, and make a ſtrong Lye
of them; then ſtrain off the clear Liquor,
and ſimmer it over the fire with a little

Turmeric

Turmeric in powder, and a very little Saffron, till it becomes pretty thick; after which set the liquor by to cool, and it is fit for use.

131. *An excellent* Perfume *for Gloves.*

TAKE Ambergrise, a drachm; the same quantity of Civet; and of Orange Flower Butter, a quarter of an ounce; mix these ingredients well, and rub them into the gloves with fine Cotton Wool, pressing the perfume into them.

132. *Or,*

TAKE of Essence of Roses, half an ounce; Oil of Cloves and Mace, of each a drachm; Frankincense, a quarter of an ounce; mix them, and lay them in papers between your gloves. Being hard pressed, the gloves will take the scent in twenty-four hours, and afterwards hardly ever lose it.

133. *An excellent Receipt to clear a tanned Complexion.*

At night going to reft, bathe the face with the Juice of Strawberries, and let it lie on the part all night, and in the morning wafh yourfelf with Chervil Water. The fkin will foon become fair and fmooth.

134. *Or,*

Wash yourfelf with the Mucilage of Linfeed, Fleawort, Gum Tragacanth, or Juice of Purflain mixed with the White of an Egg.

BREATH.

135. *To fweeten the Breath.*

At night, going to bed, chew about the quantity of a fmall Nut of fine Myrrh.

136. *Or,*

CHEW every night and morning a Clove, a piece of Florentine Orrice-root, about the fize of a fmall bean, or the fame quantity of Burnt Alum.

OILS.

137. *A Cofmetic Oil.*

TAKE a quarter of a pint of Oil of Sweet Almonds, frefh drawn; two ounces of Oil of Tartar per Deliquium; and four drops of Oil of Rhodium : mix the whole together, and make ufe of it to cleanfe and foften the fkin.

138. *Another Cofmetic Oil.*

TAKE a pint of Cream, infufe in it a few Water Lilies, Bean Flowers, and

Rofes;

Rofes; fimmer the whole together in a vapour-bath, and keep the Oil that proceeds from it in a vial, which is to be left for fome time expofed to the evening dews.

139. *Oil of Wheat.*

THIS Oil is extracted by an Iron Prefs, in the fame manner as Oil of Almonds. It is excellent for Chaps in either the lips or hands, tetterous eruptions, and rigidity of the fkin.

140. *Compound Oil, or Effence of Fennel.*

TAKE five pints of the beft French Brandy, and the fame quantity of White-Wine; three quarters of a pound of bruifed Fennel Seeds, and half an ounce of Liquorice Root fliced and bruifed. Put the whole into an alembic, clofe the mouth with Parchment, and fet it in a hot

houfe,

hou.. .. .. ho.. .. .. days; then
diftil off .. .. with an uniform
midd ing fi... What remains after the
diftillation of the Effence, and is called
the White Drops, is only fit to wafh the
hands with.

141. *To make Oil of Tuberofes and Jafmine.*

BRUISE a little the Tuberofes or Jafmine
Flowers in a marble mortar with a wooden
peftle; put them into a proper veffel, with
a fufficient quantity of Oil of Olives, and
let them ftand in the fun in a clofe ftopped
veffel twelve or fifteen days to infufe; at
the expiration of which time, fqueeze the
Oil from the Flowers. Let the Oil ftand
in the fun to fettle, then pour it clear off
the dregs. This Oil is very fragrant, and
well impregnated with the Effential Oil of
thefe Flowers. Infufe a frefh parcel of

6   Flowers,

I . . . . acred, in the fame Oil, and . . . . . as before : repeat this operation twelve or fourteen times, or even oftener if neceffary, till the Oil is fully impregnated with the flavour of the Flowers. Some people ufe Oil of Ben inftead of Sallad Oil, which in our opinion is preferable, being infinitely lefs apt to grow rancid. The Oils of Tuberofes, and Jafmine Flowers are of ufe for the Toilet on account of their fragrancy. There are cafes in which they may be fuccefsfully ufed externally by way of friction, to comfort and ftrengthen the nerves, and brace up the fkin when too much relaxed.

142. *An Oil fcented with Flowers for the Hair.*

SALLAD Oil, Oil of Sweet Almonds, and Oil of Nuts, are the only ones ufed for fcenting the hair.

Blanch

Blanch your Almonds in Hot Water, and when dry, reduce them to powder; fift them through a fine fieve, ftrewing a thin layer of Almond-powder, and one of Flowers, over the bottom of the Box lined with Tin. When the box is full, leave them in this fituation about twelve hours; then throw away the Flowers, and add frefh ones in the fame manner as before, repeating the operation every day for eight fucceffive days. When the Almond-powder is thoroughly impregnated with the fcent of the Flower made choice of, put it into a new clean Linen Cloth, and with an Iron Prefs extract the Oil, which will be ftrongly fcented with the fragrant perfume of the Flower.

ESSENTIAL OILS, or QUINTESSENCES.

143. *Essential Oil, commonly called Quint-essence of Lavender.*

FILL a cucurbit two thirds full with un-washed Lavender Flowers, pour upon them as much clear Water as will float about two inches above the Flowers. Fit to the cucurbit a head with a short neck, and lute on the refrigeratory veffel. Diftil in the common manner with a fire of fuch a degree of ftrength as will caufe the diftilled water to run off in a thick thread. The phlegm and fpirit will come over in a confiderable quantity, and the Effential Oil, with which Lavender greatly abounds, will foon appear floating on the

G   furface

furface of the Water in the receiver; which is to be feparated according to the rules of art. As foon as you perceive that no more Oil drops into the receiver, which generally happens to be the cafe a good while before the phlegm is entirely drawn off, finifh your diftillation. If you want a larger quantity of Quinteffence, empty the ftill, put frefh Flowers, and adding the phlegm and fpirit drawn off by the former diftillation, inftead of fo much common Water, diftil as before, till you have obtained a fufficient quantity. This Quinteffence poffeffes great medicinal virtues, and is particularly ferviceable in vapourifh and hyfteric diforders.

144. *To make Effence of Cinnamon.*

TAKE half a pound of Cinnamon, reduce it in a mortar to an impalpable powder,

der, put it into a very long necked matrafs, pour on it as much highly rectified Spirit of Wine as will cover the powder about an inch. Stop the matrafs with a found cork coated with bees-wax, and expofe it to the fun for a whole month, obferving to fhake it well twice a day. At the expiration of the month, uncork the matrafs, ufing the utmoft precaution not to difturb the fediment; and gently pour off the Tincture into a clean vial.

145. *To make Quinteffence of Cloves.*

TAKE a pound of Cloves, beat them in a mortar, put them into a glafs veffel, and pour on them a gallon of hot but not boiling water, cork the bottle clofe with a waxed cork, placed in a warm place, and let the Cloves infufe three weeks or a month; then empty the contents of the

bottle

bottle into a middling fized ftill, fit on a
low head with a fhort neck, and diftil in
the common manner, with a fire of fuch
a degree of fiercenefs as to make the
diftilled Water run off in a ftream, refembling a thick thread. The Quinteffence will come over with the Spirit, mixed
with a large quantity of Phlegm; but being heavier than either of thofe fubftances,
will be found precipitated to the bottom
of the receiver. Separate it in the ufual
manner, and keep it for ufe in a vial clofely
corked.   Then unlute your ftill, and
throw in the fpirituous Water that remains
after the feparation of the Quinteffence;
diftil it a fecond time, and you will
obtain a fmall quantity more, which may
be added to the former.

146. *A Cosmetic Juice.*

MAKE a hole in a Lemon, fill it with Sugar Candy, and close it nicely with leaf Gold applied over the Rind that was cut out; then roast the Lemon in hot ashes. When desirous of using the Juice, squeeze out a little through the hole, and wash the face with a napkin wetted with it. This Juice greatly cleanses the skin, and brightens the complexion.

VIRGIN's MILK.

147. *A safe and approved Cosmetic.*

TAKE equal parts of Gum Benjamin, and Storax, and dissolve them in a sufficient quantity of Spirit of Wine. The spirit will then become a reddish Tincture,

and

and exhale a very fragrant fmell. Some people add a little Balm of Gilead. Drop a few Drops into a glafs of clear Water, and the Water, by ftirring, will inftantly become milky. Ladies ufe it fuccefsfully to clear the complexion, for which purpofe nothing is better, or indeed fo innocent and fafe.

148. *Another, very eafily made.*

BEAT a quantity of Houfeleek in a marble mortar, fqueeze out the Juice and clarify it. When you want to ufe it, pour a few drops of rectified Spirit on the Juice, and it will inftantly turn milky. It is a very efficacious remedy for a pimpled face, and preferves the fkin foft and fmooth.

149. *Another.*

TAKE a half-gallon bottle, pour into it a quart of Spirit of Wine, and a pint of clear Brandy; then add a quarter of a pound of the finest **Gum Benjamin**, two ounces of Storax, half an ounce of Cinnamon, two drachms of Cloves, and a Nutmeg, all bruised, and four drops of Quintessence of Egyptian Ketmia. Carefully cork the bottle, and expose it to the sun a month; but take it within doors in rainy weather. At the month's end, gently draw off the clear Tincture; and you will have a **fragrant Milk**, which is used by pouring a few drops on a wet napkin.

150. *A Liniment to destroy Vermin.*

TAKE an ounce of Vinegar, the same quantity of Stavesacre, half an ounce of Honey, and half an ounce of Sulphur;

mix

mix into the confiftence of a foft liniment, with two ounces of Sallad Oil.

LOTIONS.

151. *A Lotion to ftrengthen the Gums, and fweeten the Breath.*

TAKE Mountain Wine, and the diftilled Water of Bramble Leaves, of each a pint ; half an ounce of Cinnamon ; a quarter of an ounce of Cloves; the fame quantity of Seville Orange-peel ; Gum Lacque and Burnt Alum, of each a drachm, all in fine powder. Having added two ounces of fine Honey, put the whole into a glafs bottle, and let them infufe on hot afhes the fpace of four days. On the fifth day fqueeze the Liquor through a thick linen cloth, and preferve it in a bottle, well corked.

When

When the gums are relaxed, and want
bracing, take a fpoonful of this Liquid,
and pour it into a glafs. Firſt uſe one
half to rince the mouth; and after retaining it a little, fpirt it out. Uſe the remainder in the fame way, rubbing the
gums with one of your fingers; and afterwards rince the mouth with warm-water.
Repeat the operation every morning, or
twice a day, if occaſion requires.

To render this remedy more efficacious,
add to the whole quantity of the Lotion
half a pint of Cinnamon Water, diſtilled
from White Wine.

The eaſtern nations, to procure a fweet
breath, to render the teeth beautifully
white, and faſten the gums, frequently
chew boiled Chio Turpentine, or Gum
Maſtic. The Indians who live beyond

G 5

the

the Ganges chew it all day long, and are so used to this habit, that they cannot without difficulty refrain from it.

The Spirituous Water of Guaiacum possesses the property of giving ease in the tooth-ache, and fastening the teeth in their sockets. The mouth is to be gargled with a quantity mixed in a glass of clear Water.

152. *Another Lotion to fasten the Teeth and sweeten the Breath.*

Pour three pints of Water into an earthen or stone jar, dip in it four different times a red hot poker, and then immediately add an ounce of bruised Cinnamon, six grains of Burnt Alum, an ounce of powdered Pomegranate Bark, three ounces of fine Honey; of Vulnerary Water, Rue Water, and Myrtle Water, each

each a quarter of a pint; and of Brandy, half a pint. The whole being well mixed, tie a wet bladder over the mouth of the jar, and let it ftand in the fun, or any warm place, for twenty-four hours; then ftrain off the Liquor through a thick linen cloth, or ftrong ftraining bag. Add to it two ounces of Spirit of Scurvy-grafs, and keep it in a bottle, well corked. It is ufed in the fame manner as the preceding Lotion.

153. *An admirable Lotion for the Complexion.*

AFTER having wafhed the face with Soap and Water, wafh yourfelf with the following lixivium. Take clear Lees prepared from Vine Afhes, and to every pound of it, add an ounce of calcined Tartar, two drachms of Gum Sandarach, and as much Gum Juniper. Let this

Lotion

Lotion dry on the face without wiping it off, and afterwards wash yourself with Imperial Water.

154. *An admirable Varnish for the Skin.*

TAKE equal parts of Lemon Juice, and Whites of new laid Eggs, beat them well together in a glazed earthen pan, which put on a flow fire, and keep the mixture constantly stirring with a wooden spatula, till it has acquired the consistence of soft butter. Keep it for use, and at the time of applying it, add a few drops of any Essence you like best. Before the face is rubbed with this varnish, it will be proper to wash with the distilled Water of rice. This is one of the best methods of rendering the complexion fair, and the skin smooth, soft, and shining.

155. *A Liniment to destroy Nits.*

TAKE Oil of Bays, Oil of Sweet Almonds, and old Hogs Lard, of each two ounces, powdered Stavesacre, and Tansy Juice, of each half an ounce; Aloes, and Myrrh, of each a quarter of an ounce, the smaller Centaury and Salt of Sulphur, of each a drachm; mix the whole into a liniment. Before you use it, wash the hair with Vinegar.

156. *A Liniment to change the Beard and Hair black.*

TAKE Oil of Costus, and Oil of Myrrh, of each an ounce and a half; mix them well in a leaden mortar, adding of Tar, the expressed Juice of Walnut Leaves, and Gum Labdanum, each half an ounce; Gall Nuts in fine powder, and Black Lead, of each a drachm and a

8   half;

half; the fame quantity of Frankincenfe; and a fufficient quantity of Mucilage of Gum Arabic, prepared with a decoction of Gall Nuts. Apply it to the head and chin after being clean fhaved.

157. *A Depilatory Liniment.*

TAKE a quarter of a pound of Quick-lime, an ounce and a half of Orpiment, an ounce of Florentine Orrice, half an ounce of Sulphur, the fame quantity of Nitre, and a pound or pint of a Lixivium made of Bean-ftalk Afhes; boil the whole to a proper confiftence, which may be known by dipping a wet feather into it. It is boiled enough when the feathery part of the quill eafily feparates from the other. Then add half an ounce of Oil of Laven-der, or any aromatic Effence, and mix into a Liniment, with which if you rub the hair that grows on any part of the

6   body,

body, it will immediately drop off. When the hair is removed, foment the part with Oil of Sweet Almonds, or Oil of Rofes.

158. *Another.*

TAKE a quarter of a pound of Gum Ivy diffolved in Vinegar, a drachm of Orpiment, a drachm of Ant Eggs, and two drachms of Gum Arabic diffolved in Juice of Henbane, in which half an ounce of Quick-lime has been boiled. Make the whole into a liniment with a fufficient quantity of Fowls Greafe, and apply a little to the part where you would wifh to deftroy the Hair, after being clean fhaved.

159. *An excellent Lip-Salve.*

TAKE an ounce of Myrrh, as much Litharge in fine powder, four ounces of Honey, two ounces of Bees-wax, and

fix

fix ounces of Oil of Rofes; mix them over a flow fire. Thofe who are inclined may add a few drops of Oil of Rhodium, and fome Leaf Gold.

160. *Or,*

TAKE Armenian Bole, Myrrh, and Cerufs in fine powder, of each an ounce; mix with a fufficient quantity of Goofe-greafe into a proper confiftence. It prefently cures chaps in any part of the body.

161. *A Liniment to promote the Growth and Regeneration of the Nails.*

TAKE two drachms of Orpiment, a drachm of Manna, the fame quantity of Aloes and Frankincenfe, and fix drachms of White Wax. Make them into a liniment, which apply to the part with a thumb-ftall.

NAILS.

162. *A certain Remedy for Whitloes; a Dif-order that frequently affects the Fingers.*

TAKE Pellitory of the Wall, cut as
fmall as poffible, and mix it with a proportionable Quantity of Hog's Lard; wrap
it up in feveral papers, one over the other,
and place it in warm afhes, which though
not hot- enough to burn the paper, yet
retain fufficient heat to roaft the Pellitory
of the Wall, and incorporate it thoroughly
with the Lard. Then fpread this Liniment on a piece of brown paper, wrap it
round the Whitloe, and apply a frefh
dreffing at leaft twice a day. That it
may give the fpeedier relief, fpread the
ointment thick.

163. *Another.*

TAKE Vine Afhes, with which make a ftrong Lee; and in this, warmed, let the finger foak a good while. To keep up an equal degree of warmth, every minute pour into the veffel a little more hot lees. Repeat this operation two or three times, and you will fpeedily find the good effect of it.

PERFUMES.

164. *Scented Tables or Paftils.*

BEAT into a fine powder, and fift through a hair fieve, a pound of the Marc or Refiduum left in the ftill, after making Angelic Water; then put it into a mortar, with a handful of frefh-gathered Rofe Leaves, and a fmall porringer full of Gum Tragacanth foftened with Rofe Water.

Beat

Beat the whole into a Paste; roll it out on a dresser with a rolling-pin, and cut it into Lozenges with a knife.

To form scented Pastils, roll up bits of this Paste in the shape of a cone, that they may stand upright, and set them by to dry. These kind of Pastils are lighted in the same manner as a candle. They consume entirely away; and, while burning, exhale a fragrant smoke.

165. *A pleasant Perfume.*

TAKE a drachm of Musk, four Cloves, four ounces of Lavender-seed, a drachm and a half of Civet, and half a drachm of Ambergrise; heat your pestle and mortar, and rub the Musk, Cloves, and Lavender-seeds together, with a lump of Loaf Sugar and a wine-glass full of Angelic or Rose-water.

water. Take a handful of powder, and incorporate it well with this mixture, then fift it through a fieve; add two or three pounds more powder, or even a larger quantity, till the perfume is brought to a proper degree of ſtrength. As to the Civet, put it on the end of a hot peſtle, and rub it well with a handful of powder; after which add, by little and little, fix pounds of powder; then fift the whole through a hair fieve to incorporate it with the other perfumed powder. The Ambergriſe muſt be well rubbed in the mortar; and by degrees two pounds of powder, either white or grey, muſt be added to it, till the Ambergriſe is thoroughly incorporated with the pow- der; then fift through a hair fieve, and mix all the three powders toge- ther. This perfume is to be kept in a

Leather Bag, the seams of which are well sewed with waxed thread.

166. *Common perfumed Powder.*

TAKE Florentine Orrice, a pound, dried Rose Leaves, a pound; Gum Benjamin, two ounces; Storax, an ounce; Yellow Sanders, an ounce and a half; Cloves, two drachms; and a little Lemon Peel : reduce the whole to a fine powder, and mix with it twenty pounds of Starch, or rather of grey or white powder; incorporate them well, and sift them through a lawn sieve.

167. *A Cassolette.*

INCORPORATE the Powders of Florentine Orrice, Storax, Benjamin and other aromatics, with Orange-flower Water; and put this Paste into a little Silver or Copper Box lined with Tin. When you have a mind to use this perfume, set the Box on

a gentle

a gentle fire, or on hot aſhes, and it will exhale a moſt delightful odour.

168. *To perfume a Houſe, and purify the*
Air.

TAKE a root of Angelica, dry it in an oven, or before the fire, then bruiſe it well and infuſe it four or five days in White Wine Vinegar. When you uſe it, lay it upon a brick made red hot, and repeat the operation ſeveral times.

169. *A Perfume to ſcent Powder.*

TAKE a drachm of Muſk, four ounces of Lavender Seeds, a drachm and a half of Civet, and half a drachm of Ambergriſe. Beat the whole together into powder, and ſift through a hair ſieve. Keep this perfume in a box that ſhuts very cloſe, to ſcent powder with, according to your fancy.

P A S T I L S.

170. *An excellent Composition to perfume a Room agreeably.*

TAKE four ounces of Gum Benjamin, two ounces of Storax, and a quarter of an ounce of Aloes-wood. When these ingredients have been well bruised, simmer them about half an hour over a slow fire, in a glazed earthen pipkin, with as much Rose-water as will cover them, and then strain off the liquor for use. Dry the Residuum or Marc, and pulverize it in a warm mortar with a pound of Charcoal. Dissolve some Gum Tragacanth in the reserved Liquor, then add to your powder a drachm of fine Oriental Musk dissolved in a little Rose-water, and form the whole into a Paste, of which make pastils about the length and thickness of the little finger, narrower at top than at bottom,

that

that they may ftand firm and upright.
When they are thoroughly dry, light
them at the narrow end, and let them
burn till they are wholly confumed. While
burning they afford an exquifite perfume.
To render the perfume ftill higher, add fix
grains of Ambergrife.

171. *Or,*

PULVERIZE together two ounces of Gum
Benjamin, half an ounce of Storax, a drachm
of Aloes-wood, twenty grains of fine Civet, a little Sea Coal, and Loaf Sugar;
boil the whole in a fufficient quantity of
Rofe-water, to the confiftence of a ftiff
pafte. If you are defirous of having your
paftils higher flavoured, add twelve grains
of Ambergrife juft before you take the
compofition off the fire; and the ingredients being thoroughly mixed, form them
into paftils.

172. *Fragrant Paſtils made uſe of by way of Fumigation.*

TAKE the pureſt Labdanum and Gum Benjamin, of each two ounces; Storax and dry Balſam of Peru, of each three quarters of an ounce; choice Myrrh, half a drachm; Gum Tacamahac, a quarter of an ounce; Olibanum, a drachm; Liquid Balſam of Peru, half an ounce; Ambergriſe, a quarter of an ounce; Muſk and Civet, of each a ſcruple; Eſſential Oil of Rhodium, thirty drops; Eſſential Oils of Orange-flowers, Lemons, and Bergamot, of each four drops; Gum Lacque, in fine powder, two ounces and a half; Caſcarilla, Aloes-wood, Roſe-wood, St. Lucia-wood, Yellow Sanders, and Cinnamon, all powdered, of each a drachm. With the aſſiſtance of a vapour-bath reduce them to a maſs, which form into paſtils in the uſual way.

H

173. *Paſtils of Roſes.*

PULVERIZE a pound of the Marc or Reſiduum left in the ſtill after making Angelica
Water; likewiſe a large handful of Roſes;
and with a ſufficient quantity of Gum Tragacanth diſſolved in Roſe-water, beat them
into a ſtiff paſte, which is to be rolled out
upon a marble with a rolling-pin, and
cut into Lozenges, or formed into paſtils.
If you have a mind to ornament them,
cover them with Leaf Gold or Silver.

PASTES.

174. *Paſte of dried Almonds to cleanſe the Skin.*

BEAT any quantity you pleaſe, of Sweet
and Bitter Almonds in a marble mortar,
and while beating, pour on them a little
Vinegar in a ſmall ſtream to prevent their
turning

turning oily : then add two drachms of
Storax in fine powder, two ounces of
White Honey, and two Yolks of Eggs
boiled hard; mix the whole into a paſte.

175. *Soft Almond Paſte.*

BLANCH in warm water any quantity
of Bitter Almonds, leave them to grow
dry, and then beat them in a marble mortar with a little Milk, to form them into a
paſte.   To prevent their turning oily,
afterwards add the Crumb of a light White
Loaf ſoaked in Milk.   Beat it with the
Almonds till they are incorporated into an
uniform maſs ; then put the whole into
a kettle, with ſome freſh Milk, and let
them ſimmer over a gentle fire ; keeping the
compoſition ſtirring, till it is boiled into a
ſoft paſte.

176. *Paste for the Hands.*

TAKE Sweet Almonds, half a pound;
White Wine Vinegar, Brandy, and Spring
Water, of each two quarts; two ounces
of Crumb of Bread, and the Yolks of
two Eggs. Blanch and beat the Almonds,
moistening them with the Vinegar; add
the Crumb of Bread soaked in the Brandy,
and mix it with the Almonds and Yolks
of Egg, by repeated Trituration. Then
pour in the Water, and simmer the whole
over a slow fire, keeping the composition
continually stirring, till it has acquired a
proper consistence.

177. *Or,*

TAKE Bitter and Sweet Almonds
blanched, of each two ounces; Pine-nuts,
and the four Cold Seeds, of each an ounce;
beat the whole together in a marble mortar
with

with the Yolks of two Eggs, and the Crumb of a small Wheaten Loaf. Moisten the mass with White Wine Vinegar, put it into a deep pan, simmer it over a slow fire, and when the paste ceases sticking to the pan, it is sufficiently boiled.

178. Or,

TAKE blanched Almonds, a pound; Pine-nuts, four ounces; beat them together into a paste with the addition of two ounces of Loaf Sugar, an ounce of the finest Honey, the same quantity of Bean Flower, and half a gill of Brandy. This paste may be scented with the Essences of Cloves, Lemons, Bergamot, Jasmine, Rhodium, Orange Flowers, &c. or with a few grains of Musk, Civet, or a few drops of Essence of Ambergrise, for persons who have no aversion to those perfumes.

H 3

179. *Or,*

Beat half a pound of blanched Almonds, with half an ounce of Yellow Sanders, half an ounce of Florentine Orrice, and an ounce of Calamus Aromaticus, in fine powder; pour on them gradually an ounce of Rofe-water, and then add half a Pippin fliced fmall, a quarter of a pound of ftale Crumb of White Bread fifted fine, and knead the whole into a pafte with two ounces of Gum Tragacanth diffolved in Rofe-water.

180. *Or,*

Beat fome peeled apples (having firft taken out the Cores) in a marble mortar, with Rofe-water, and White Wine, of each equal parts. Add fome Crumb of Bread, blanched Almonds, and a little White

White Soap; and fimmer the whole over a flow fire till it acquires a proper confiftence.

181. *Or,*

INFUSE fome blanched Almonds, two or three hours, in Goat's or Cow's Milk, and beat them into a pafte. Strain the infufion through a linen cloth with a ftrong preffure, and add to the ftrained Liquor half a pound of the Crumb of White Bread, a quarter of a pound of Borax, and as much Burnt Roch Alum. Simmer the whole together, and when almoft boiled enough, add an ounce of Spermaceti. Stir the compofition well with a fpatula to prevent it from burning to the bottom of the pan; and let it fimmer but very gently.

H 4

182. *Or,*

DRY, before the fire, half a pound of Bitter Almonds blanched, then beat them in a marble mortar as fine as poffible, and add a little boiled Milk to prevent the Almonds from turning oily. Beat in the fame manner the Crumb of two French Bricks, with four Yolks of Eggs boiled hard, and with the addition of fome frefh Milk knead them into a pafte, which incorporate with that of the Almonds.

POMATUMS.

183. *Cold Cream, or Pomatum for the Complexion.*

TAKE White Wax and Spermaceti, of each a drachm; Oil of Sweet Almonds, two ounces; Spring Water, an ounce and a half;

a half; melt the Wax and Spermaceti together in the Oil of Almonds, in a glazed earthen pipkin, over hot afhes, or in a vapour-bath; pour the folution into a marble mortar, and ftir it about with a wooden peftle, till it grow cold, and feem quite fmooth; then mix the Water gradually, and keep ftirring, till the whole is incorporated. This pomatum becomes extremely white and light by the agitation, and very much refembles cream, from its fimilitude to which it has obtained its name.

This pomatum is an excellent cofmetic, and renders the fkin fupple and fmooth. Some add a little Balm of Gilead to heighten its virtue; and it is fometimes fcented, by ufing Rofe-water or Orange-flower Water in the preparation, inftead of Spring-water, or with a few drops of any

H 5   Effence,

Effence, as fancy directs. It is also very good to prevent marks in the face from the Small-pox; in which laft cafe, a little powder of Saffron, or fome deficcative powder, fuch as Flowers of Zinc or French Chalk, is ufually added. Keep it for ufe in a large gallypot tied over with a bladder.

184. *Cucumber Pomatum.*

Take Hog's Lard, a pound; ripe Melons, and Cucumbers, of each three pounds, Verjuice, half a pint; two pippins pared, and a pint of Cow's Milk. Slice the Melons, Cucumbers, and Apples, having firft pared them; bruife them in the Verjuice, and, together with the Milk and Hog's Lard, put them into an alembic. Let them infufe in a vapour-bath eight or ten hours; then fqueeze out the Liquor through a ftraining cloth while the mixture is hot,

and

and expofe it to the cold air, or fet it in a cool place to congeal. Afterwards pour off the watery part that fubfides, and wafh it in feveral Waters, till the laft remains perfectly clear. Melt the pomatum again in a vapour-bath feveral times, to feparate from it all its humid particles, and every extraneous fubftance; otherwife it will foon grow rancid. Keep it for ufe in a gallypot tied over with a bladder.

185. *Or,*

A more fimple Cucumber Pomatum may be made by fimmering together Hog's Lard and pared Cucumbers cut in thin flices. With refpect to the reft of the pro-cefs, follow the method laid down for pre-paring Lip-falve; and keep this pomatum in the fame manner as the former.

H 6 Both

Both thefe pomatums are good Cofme-
tics; they foften the fkin, and preferve it
cool and fmooth.

186. *Lavender Pomatum.*

TAKE two pounds and a half of Hog's
Lard, ten pounds of Lavender Flowers,
and a quarter of a pound of Virgin's
Wax; put two pounds of picked Lavender Flowers into a proper veffel with the
Hog's Lard, and knead them with your
hands into as uniform a pafte as poffible.
Put this mixture into a pewter, tin, or
ftone pot, and cork it tight; place the
veffel in a vapour-bath, and let it ftand fix
hours; at the expiration of which time,
ftrain the mixture through a coarfe linen
cloth, with the affiftance of a prefs.
Throw away the Lavender Flowers as
ufelefs, pour the melted Lard back into
the fame pot, and add four pounds of
frefh

fresh Lavender Flowers. Stir the Lard
and Flowers together while the Lard is
in a liquid state, in order to mix them
thoroughly; and repeat the former procefs.
Continue to act in this manner till the
whole quantity of Lavender Flowers is
ufed. Then fet in a cool place the pomatum feparated from the Lavender Flowers,
that it may congeal; pour off the brown
aqueous juice extracted from them; and
wash the Pomatum in feveral waters, ftirring it with a wooden fpatula, to feparate
any remaining watery particles, till the
laft water remains perfectly colourlefs.
Then melt the Pomatum in a vapour-bath,
and keep it in that ftate about an hour, in
a veffel well corked; leaving it afterwards
to congeal. Repeat this laft operation
till the aqueous particles are entirely extracted when the Wax muft be added, and
the Pomatum having been again melted, in a

6   vapour-

vapour-bath, in a veſſel cloſely corked, be ſuffered to congeal as before. When properly prepared, fill it into gallypots, and tye the mouths over with wet bladders, to prevent the air from penetrating.

This Pomatum is extremely fragrant, but is uſed only for dreſſing the hair.

In the ſame manner are prepared, Orange-flower Pomatum, Jaſmine Pomatum, and all Pomatums made of odoriferous flowers. Common Pomatum ſcented with the eſſences of any ſuch flowers, may be uſed as a good ſuccedaneum.

187. LIP-SALVES.

Take three ounces of Oil of Almonds, three quarters of an ounce of Spermaceti, and a quarter of an ounce of Virgin's gin's Wax; melt them together over a flow fire, mixing with them a little of the powder of Alkanet Root. Keep ſtirring till cold, and then add a few drops of Oil of Rhodium.

188. *Or,*

TAKE prepared Tutty and Oil of Eggs, of each equal parts; mix, and apply them to the lips, after waſhing the latter with Barley or Plantane Water.

189. *Or,*

PLACE over a chafing-diſh of coals, in a glazed earthen pan, a quarter of a pound of the beſt freſh Butter, and an ounce of Virgin's Wax; melt them together; when thoroughly melted, throw in the Stones of half a bunch of ripe Black Grapes, with ſome Alkanet Roots a little bruiſed. Sim-mer theſe ingredient together for a quarter

of

of an hour; afterwards ftrain the mixture through a fine linen cloth; and pour into your pomatum, which muft be again fet on the fire, a fpoonful of Orange-flower Water. Having let them fimmer together a little while, take the pan off the fire, and keep the pomatum ftirring till it become quite cold. It will keep a long while, and is a perfect cure for chapped lips.

190. *A Yellow Lip-Salve.*

TAKE Yellow Bee's Wax, two ounces and a half; Oil of Sweet Almonds, a quarter of a pint; melt the Wax in the Oil, and let the mixture ftand till it become cold, when it acquires a pretty ftiff confiftence. Scrape it into a marble mortar, and rub it with a wooden peftle, to render it perfectly fmooth. Keep it for ufe in a gallypot, clofely covered.

It is emollient and lenient; of courfe good for chaps in the lips, hands, or nipples; and preferves the fkin foft and fmooth.

A Cruft of Bread applied hot, is an efficacious remedy for pimples that rife on the lips, in confequence of having drank out of a glafs after an uncleanly perfon.

191. *A Scarlet Lip-Salve.*

TAKE Hog's Lard wafhed in Rofe-water, half a pound; Red Rofes and Damafk Rofes bruifed, a quarter of a pound; knead them together and let them lie in that ftate two days. Then melt the Hog's Lard, and ftrain it from the Rofes. Add a frefh quantity of the latter, knead them in the Hog's Lard, and let them lie together two days as before; then gently fimmer the mixture in a vapour-bath.

Prefs

Preſs out the Lard, and keep it for uſe in the ſame manner as other Lip-ſalves.

192. *Or,*

TAKE an ounce of Oil of Sweet Almonds cold drawn, a drachm of freſh Mutton Suet, and a little bruiſed Alkanet Root; ſimmer the whole together. Inſtead of Oil of Sweet Almonds you may uſe Oil of Jaſmine, or the Oil of any other Flower, if you chooſe the Lip-ſalve ſhould have a fragrant ſcent.

193. *Or,*

TAKE Oil of Violets, and the expreſſed Juice of Mallows, of each an ounce and a half; Gooſe Greaſe and Veal Marrow, of each a quarter of an ounce; Gum Tragacanth, a drachm and a half; melt the whole over a gentle fire.

194. *Or,*

TAKE half a pound of fresh Butter, a quarter of a pound of Bee's Wax, four or five ounces of cleansed Black Grapes, and about an ounce of bruised Alkanet Root; simmer them together over a slow fire till the Wax is wholly dissolved, and the mixture become of a bright red colour; then strain, and set it by for use.

195. *Or,*

TAKE Deer or Goat's Suet, six ounces; Hog's Lard, four ounces: cut them into little bits, and wash them five or six different times in White Wine; then by hard pressure squeeze out every drop of the Wine. Melt the fats in a new-glazed earthen pan with half an ounce of Orrice Roots cut in thin slices, a grated Nutmeg, two or three Pippins pared and sliced thin, a pint a pint of Rofe-water, an ounce of Bee's Wax, and half an ounce of bruifed Cloves. Simmer the whole over a flow fire about half an hour; then ftrain through a linen cloth into a pan half full of clean Water. Let the pomatum remain in the pan till cold, then wafh it well, and beat it in a marble mortar with two ounces of White Wax, till they be thoroughly incorporated. Apply a little to the lips every night going to reft; and rub it upon the hands every night and morning.

196. *White Pomatum.*

TAKE an ounce of Florentine Orrice-root, half an ounce of Calamus Aromaticus, and as much Gum Benjamin, a quarter of an ounce of Rofe-wood, and a quarter of an ounce of Cloves. Bruife the whole into a grofs powder, tie it up in a piece of linen, and fimmer it in a

vapour-

vapour-bath, with two pounds and a half of Hog's Lard well wafhed; add a couple of Pippins pared and cut into fmall bits, four ounces of Rofe water, and two ounces of Orange-flower Water. After the ingredients have fimmered together a little while, ftrain off the Liquor gently, and let the Pomatum ftand till cold; then put it by for ufe in the fame manner as other pomatums.

197. *Red Pomatum*

Is made by adding to the above more or lefs Alkanet Root bruifed, according to the depth of colour you would wifh to impart. Simmer the Pomatum and Alkanet together, ftirring the mixture with a wooden fpatula, till the Pomatum is fufficiently tinged; then ftrain it from the Roots, and fet it by for ufe.

STEEP in clear Water a pound of a Boar's Cheek till it becomes tolerably white, drain it quite dry, and put it into a new-glazed earthen pan with two or three pared Pippins quartered, an ounce and a half of the four Cold Seeds bruised, and a slice of Veal about the size of the palm of one's hand. Boil the whole together in a vapour-bath for four hours, then with a strong cloth squeeze out your pomatum into an earthen dish placed upon hot ashes; adding to it an ounce of White Wax, and an ounce of Oil of Sweet Almonds. Stir the pomatum well with a spatula till it become cold.

199. *A Pomatum for Wrinkles.*

TAKE Juice of White Lily Roots and fine Honey, of each two ounces; melted White Wax, an ounce; incorporate the whole together, and make a pomatum. It should be applied every night, and not be wiped off till the next morning.

200. *Another for the same Intention.*

TAKE fix new-laid Eggs, boil them hard, take out the Yolks, and fill the cavities with Myrrh, and powdered Sugar Candy, of each equal parts. Join the Whites together neatly, and fet them on a plate before the fire; mixing the Liquor that exfudes from them with an ounce of Hog's Lard. This pomatum muft be applied in the morning, and be fuffered to dry upon the fkin, which is afterwards to be wiped with a clean fine napkin.

20.. Or,

TAKE half an ounce of Sallad Oil, an ounce of Oil of Tartar, half an ounce of Mucilage of Quince Seeds, three quarters of an ounce of Cerufs, thirty grains of Borax, and the fame quantity of Sal Gem. Stir the whole together for fome time in a little earthen difh, with a wooden fpatula, and apply it in the fame manner as the former compofition.

202. *Pomatum for a red or pimpled Face.*

TAKE two pared Apples, Celery, and Fennel, of each a handful; and Barley Meal, a quarter of an ounce. Simmer the whole together a quarter of an hour in a gill of Rofe-water; then add an ounce of fine Barley Meal, the Whites of four new-laid Eggs, and an ounce of Deer's Suet.

Strain

Strain through a canvas bag into a dish that contains a little Rose-water; wash the pomatum well in the Rose-water, and afterwards beat it in a mortar perfectly smooth. This pomatum is to be applied frequently through the day, to remove the redness of the face, pimples, and even freckles; but to answer the last mentioned purpose, it must be continued till they are entirely effaced. To prevent their return, the person must avoid the intense heat of the sun, and hot drying winds for some time.

203. *A Pomatum for the Skin.*

TAKE Oil of White Poppy Seeds, and of the four Cold Seeds, of each a gill; Spermaceti, three quarters of an ounce; White Wax, an ounce: mix them into a pomatum according to the rules of art.

I

A great

A great quantity of a fubftance refembling Butter is extracted from the Cocoa Tree, which is excellent to mollify and nourifh the fkin, and has long been ufed for this purpofe amongft the Spanifh Creolian women.

204. *Pomatum to make the Hair grow in a bald Part, and thicken the Hair.*

TAKE Hen's Fat, Oil of Hempfeed, and Honey, of each a quarter of a pound; melt them together in an earthen pipkin, and keep the mixture ftirring with a wooden fpatula, till cold. This pomatum, to obtain the defired effect, muft be rubbed on the part eight days fucceffively.

205. *Another Pomatum for the Hair.*

CUT into small pieces a sufficient quantity of Hog's Cheek, steep it eight or ten days in clean Water, which be careful to change three times a day, and every time the Water is changed, stir it well with a spatula to make the flesh white. Drain the flesh dry, and putting it into a new earthen pipkin, with a pint of Rose-water, and a Lemon stuck with Cloves, simmer them over the fire till the skum looks reddish. Skim this off, and removing the pipkin from the fire, strain the Liquor. When it has cooled, take off the fat; beat it well with cold Water, which change two or three times as occasion may require; the last time using Rose-water instead of common Water. Drain the Pomatum dry, and scent it with

I 2   Violets,

Violets, Tuberoses, Orange Flowers, Jaf-mine, Jonquils a-la Reine, &c. in the fol-lowing manner.

206. *Manner of Scenting Pomatums for the Hair.*

SPREAD your Pomatum about an inch thick upon feveral difhes or plates, ftrew-ing the flowers you make choice of on one difh, and covering them with another. Change the Flowers for frefh ones every twelve hours, and continue to purfue this method for ten or twelve days; mixing the pomatum well, and fpreading it out every time that frefh Flowers are added. It will foon acquire a fragrant fcent, and may be ufed in what manner you think proper. It is good for almoft every cofmetic purpofe, but more particularly for the hair, which it nourifhes, ftrengthens, preferves, and thickens.

207. *Orange-Flower Pomatum.*

TAKE two pounds and a half of Hog's Lard, and three pounds of Orange Flowers ; mix them together in a marble mortar; then put the mixture into an earthen veffel with fome Water, and place it in a vapour-bath, where let it ftand till the Lard is melted, and floats above the Flowers. When it has ftood till cold, pour away the Water, and fimmer in the ufual manner, with three pounds of frefh Orange Flowers. Repeat the fame operation twice more with two pounds of Orange Flowers each time ; and the laft time, while the mixture ftands in infufion, add a gill of Orange-flower Water. Strain through a hair fieve held over an earthen difh ; drain off the Water thoroughly when cold, and keep the Pomatum in a dry

I 3 place,

place, in a gallypot clofe tied over with a bladder.

In the fame manner are prepared Jaf-mine, Jonquil, Tuberofe, Lavender Po-matums, and all pomatums fcented with Flowers.

208. *Sultana Pomatum.*

THIS pomatum is made of Balfam of Mecca, Spermaceti, and Oil of Sweet Almonds cold drawn. It clears and pre-ferves the complexion, and is of ufe for red pimpled faces.

209. *A fweet fmelling Perfume.*

TAKE a pound of frefh-gathered Orange Flowers, of common Rofes, Lavender Seeds, and Mufk Rofes, each half a pound;

pound; of Sweet Marjoram Leaves, and Clove-july-flowers picked, each a quarter of a pound; of Thyme, three ounces; of Myrtle Leaves, and Melilot Stalks stripped of their Leaves, each two ounces; of Rosemary Leaves, and Cloves bruised, each an ounce; of Bay Leaves, half an ounce.

Let these ingredients be mixed in a large pan covered with parchment, and be exposed to the heat of the sun during the whole summer; for the first month stirring them every other day with a stick, and taking them within doors in rainy weather. Towards the end of the season, they will afford an excellent composition for a perfume; which may be rendered yet more fragrant, by adding a little scented Cypress-powder, mixed with coarse Violet-powder.

I 4

210. *Another for the same Purpose.*

TAKE Orange Flowers, a pound; common Rofes picked without the Yellow Pedicles, a pound; Clove-july-flowers picked with the White End of their Leaves cut off, half a pound; Marjoram, and Myrtle Leaves picked, of each half a pound; Mufk Rofes, Thyme, Lavender, Rofemary, Sage, Chamomile, Melilot, Hyffop, Sweet Bafil, and Balm, of each two ounces; fifteen or twenty Bay Leaves, two or three handfuls of Jafmine, as many little Green Oranges, and half a pound of Salt. Put them in a proper veffel, and leave them together a whole month, carefully obferving to ftir the mixture well twice a day with a wooden fpatula or fpoon.

At

At the month's end, add twelve ounces of Florentine Orrice-root in fine powder, and the same quantity of powdered Benjamin; of Cloves, and Cinnamon finely powdered, each two ounces; Mace, Storax, Calamus Aromaticus, all in fine powder, and Cyprefs-powder, of each an ounce; Yellow Sanders and Cyprus or Sweet Flag, of each three quarters of an ounce. Mix the whole thoroughly, by stirring, and you will have a very fragrant perfume.

POWDERS.

211. *Orange-Flower Powder.*

Put half a pound of Orange Flowers into a box that contains twelve pounds and a half of powdered Starch; mix them well with the Starch, and stir the mixture at intervals, to prevent the Flowers

I 5 from

from heating. At the expiration of twenty-four hours, remove the old flowers, and mix with the Starch the same quantiiy of fresh Orange Flowers. Continue acting in this manner for three days together, and if you think the perfume not sufficiently strong, add fresh Flowers once or twice more. The box must be kept close shut, as well after as during the operation.

212.   *Jonquil Powder.*

TAKE of Starch Powder and Jonquil Flowers, in the same proportion as in the preceding article; strew the Flowers among the Powder, and at the expiration of twenty hours, sift it through a coarse sieve. Then throw away the Flowers, and add to the Powder the same quantity of fresh Flowers. Continue this method four or five days, observing never to touch

touch the Powder while the Flowers lie mixed with it; and the former will hence acquire a very agreeable perfume.

In the fame manner are prepared, Hyacinth, Mufk Rofe, and Damafk Rofe Powders, &c.

213. *Coarfe Violet Powder.*

BEAT feparately into coarfe Powder the following ingredients, viz. half a pound of dried Orange Flowers; of Lemon-peel dried, Yellow Sanders, Mufk Rofes, and Gum Benjamin, each a quarter of a pound; Lavender Tops dried, three ounces; of Rofe Wood, Calamus Aromaticus, and Storax, each two ounces; an ounce of Sweet Marjoram, half an ounce of Cloves, two pounds of Florentine Orrice-root, and a pound of dried Provence Rofes; mix the whole together. When you want to fill

16 bags

bags with this powder, mix a drachm of Muſk and half a drachm of Civet, with a little Mucilage of Gum Tragacanth made with Angelic Water, and a little Sweet-ſcented Water, and rub the inſide of the bag over with the compoſition, before you fill it with the Violet Powder.

214. *Another coarſe Violet Powder.*

Mix together a pound of Florentine Orrice-roots, half a pound of dried Orange Flowers, a quarter of a pound of Yellow Sanders; of Coriander Seeds, Sweet Flag, and of the Marc or Reſiduum left after making Angelic Water, each two ounces; an ounce and a half of Calamus Aromaticus, and an ounce of Cloves; bruiſe the whole into a coarſe Powder, and keep it for uſe in a jar, cloſe ſtopped.

215. *Jasmine Powder.*

POWDER French Chalk, sift it through a fine sieve, put it in a box, and strew on it a quantity of Jasmine Flowers; shut down the lid close, and add fresh Flowers every four and twenty hours. When the Powder is well impregnated with the scent of Jasmine, rub together a few grains of Civet, Ambergrise, and a little white Sugar Candy, and mix them with the Powder.

216. *Ambrette Powder.*

TAKE six ounces of Bean Flour, and the same quantity of worm-eaten Wood, four ounces of Cyprus Wood, two ounces of Yellow Sanders, two ounces of Gum Benjamin, an ounce and a half of Storax, a quarter of an ounce of Calamus Aromaticus,

Aromaticus, aud as much Labdanum; beat the whole into a very fine powder, and fift it through a lawn fieve. Add four grains of Ambergrife, and half an ounce of Mahaleb or Mufk Seeds; mix them with the reft of the powder, and keep the whole in a bottle clofe ftopped for ufe. You may put any quantity you pleafe of this Perfume into common powder, to give it an agreeable flavour.

217. *Cyprus Powder.*

FILL a linen bag with Oak Mofs, fteep it in water, which change frequently, and afterwards dry the Mofs in the fun. Beat it to powder, and fprinkle it with Rofe-water; then dry it again, fift it through a fine fieve, and mix with it a fmall quan-tity of any of the preceding powders.

218. *Another Cyprus Powder more fra-*
grant.

WASH Oak Mofs feveral times in pure
water and dry it thoroughly; then fprinkle
over it Orange Flower and Rofe-water,
and fpread it thin upon a hurdle to dry.
Afterwards place under it a chafing-difh,
in which burn fome Storax and Benjamin.
Repeat this operation till the Mofs becomes
well perfumed; then beat it to fine powder, and to every pound add a quarter of
an ounce of Mufk, and as much Civet.

219. *Perfumed Powder.*

TAKE a pound of Florentine Orrice-
root, two ounces of Gum Benjamin, a
pound of dried Rofes, an ounce of Storax,
an ounce and a half of Yellow Sanders,
a quarter of an ounce of Cloves, and a
fmall

small quantity of Lemon-peel; beat the whole together into fine powder, and then add twenty pounds of Starch-powder. Sift through a lawn sieve; and colour the powder according to your fancy.

220. *The White Powder that enters into the Composition of the Delightful Perfume.*

TAKE a pound of Florentine Orrice-root, twelve Cuttle-fish Bones, eight pounds of Starch, and a handful of Sheep or Bullock's Bones calcined to whiteness; beat the whole into a powder, and sift it through a fine hair sieve.

221. *Prepared Powder.*

POUR a quart of Brandy, or an ounce of highly rectified Spirit of Wine, on a pound or a pound and a half of Starch, mix them together; then dry the Starch,

beat

beat it to powder, and fift it through a
fine lawn fieve. If you pleafe you may add
a little powder of Florentine Orrice-root.

222. *A Powder to nourifh the Hair.*

Take Roots of the Sweet Flag, Calamus Aromaticus, and Red Rofes dried,
of each an ounce and a half; Gum Benjamin, an ounce; Aloes Wood, three quarters of an ounce; Red Coral prepared, and
Amber prepared, of each half an ounce;
Bean Flour, a quarter of a pound, Florentine Orrice-roots, half a pound; mix the
whole together, then beat into a fine powder, and add to it five grains of Mufk, and
the fame quantity of Civet. This powder greatly promotes the regeneration of
the hair, and ftrengthens and nourifhes
its roots. The property of enlivening the
imagination, and helping the memory is
alfo attributed to it.

223. *Common Powder.*

THE beſt Starch dried is generally the baſis of all Hair-powders : as are, ſometimes, worm-eaten or rotten Wood, dried Bones, or Bones calcined to whiteneſs, which are ſifted through a fine hair ſieve after they have been beaten to powder. This kind of Powder readily takes any ſcent, particularly that of Florentine Orrice, a root which naturally poſſeſſes a violet ſmell. Of theſe Roots, the whiteſt and foundeſt are made choice of ; they are to be powdered as fine as poſſible, and this can only be done during the ſummer.

224. *White Powder.*

TAKE four pounds of Starch, half a pound of Florentine Orrice-root, ſix Cuttle-fiſh Bones ; Ox Bones and Sheeps Bones

Bones calcined to whitenefs, of each half a handful; beat the whole together, and fift the Powder through a very fine fieve.

225. *Grey Powder*.

To the Refiduum of the preceding add a little Starch and Wood-afhes in fine powder; rub them together in a mortar fome time, and then fift through a fine hair fieve.

226. *Another*.

TAKE the Marc or Refiduum of the White Powder, mix with it a little Starch, Yellow Ochre, and Wood-afhes or Baker's Coals to colour it. Beat the whole well in a mortar, then fift it through a hair fieve. Beat the coarfer parts over again, and fift a fecond time; repeating thefe operations till all the compofition has paffed through the fieve.

227. *Flaxen coloured Powder.*

ADD to the White Powder a very little Yellow Ochre. The White Powder may be tinged of any colour, by adding ingredients of the colour you fancy.

228. *Bean Flour.*

GRIND any quantity of Beans, and sift the Meal through a very fine lawn sieve. It will take no other scent than that of Florentine Orrice.

229. *To sweeten the Breath.*

ROLL up a little ball of Gum Tragacanth, scent it with some odoriferous Essence or Oil, and hold it in the mouth. A little Musk may be added to the ball while rolling up, where that perfume is not disagreeable.

230. *Or,*

AFTER having eat Garlic or Onions, chew a little raw Parſley. It will infallibly take away their offenſive ſmell.

231. *A Remedy for ſcorbutic Gums.*

BRUISE Cinquefoil in a marble mortar, ſqueeze out the Juice, warm it over the fire, and rub the Gums with it every night and morning.

232. *A Remedy for Moiſt Feet.*

TAKE twenty pounds of Lee made of the Aſhes of the Bay Tree, three handfuls of Bay Leaves, a handful of Sweet Flag, with the ſame quantity of Calamus Aromaticus, and Dittany of Crete; boil the whole together for ſome time, then ſtrain off the liquor, and add two quarts of Wine.

Wine. Steep your feet in this bath an hour every day, and in a fhort time they will no longer exhale a difagreeable fmell.

F L E A S.

233. *A certain Method of deftroying Fleas.*

Sprinkle the room with a decoction of Arfmart, Bitter Apple, Briar Leaves, or Cabbage Leaves; or fmoke it with burnt Thyme or Pennyroyal.

234. *Or,*

Put Tanfy Leaves about different parts of the bed, viz. under the matrafs, or between the blankets.

235. *Or,*

Rub the bed-posts well with a strong decoction of Elder Leaves.

236. *Or,*

Mercurial Ointment, or a fumigation of Pennyroyal Leaves, or of Brimstone, infallibly destroys Fleas; as likewise do the fresh Leaves of Pennyroyal, tied up in a bag, and laid upon the bed.

WRINKLES.

237. *A Secret to take away Wrinkles.*

Heat an Iron Shovel red hot, throw on it some Powder of Myrrh, and receive the smoke on your face, covering the head with a napkin to prevent its being dissipated. Repeat this operation three

times,

8

times, then heat the Shovel again, and when fiery hot pour on it a mouthful of White Wine. Receive the vapour of the Wine also on your face, and repeat it three times. Continue this method every night and morning as long as you find occasion.

CARMINES.

238. *A Rouge for the Face.*

ALKANET Root strikes a beautiful red when mixed with Oils or Pomatums. A Scarlet or Rose-coloured Ribband wetted with Water or Brandy, gives the Cheeks, if rubbed with it, a beautiful bloom that can hardly be distinguished from the natural colour. Others only use a Red Sponge, which tinges the cheeks of a fine carnation colour.

239. *Another.*

TAKE Brazil Wood Shavings, and Roch Alum, beat them together into a coarfe powder, and boil in a fufficient quantity of Red Wine, till two thirds of the Liquor are confumed. When this decoction has ftood till cold, rub a little on the cheeks with a bit of cotton.

240. *The Turkifh Method of preparing Carmine.*

INFUSE, during three or four days, in a large jar filled with White Wine Vinegar, a pound of Brazil Wood Shavings of Fernambuca, having firft beaten them to a coarfe powder; afterwards boil them together half an hour; then ftrain off the Liquor through a coarfe linen cloth, fet it

K   again

again upon the fire, and having diffolved half a pound of Alum in White Wine Vinegar, mix both Liquors together, aud ftir the mixture well with a fpatula. The fcum that rifes is the Carmine; fkim it off carefully, and dry it for ufe.

Carmine may alfo be made with Cochineal, or Red Sanders, inftead Brazil Wood.

241. *A Liquid Rouge that exactly imitates Nature.*

TAKE a pint of good Brandy, and infufe in it half an ounce of Gum Benjamin, an ounce of Red Sanders, and half an ounce of Brazil Wood, both in coarfe powder; with half an ounce of Roch Alum. Cork the bottle tight, fhake it well every day, and at the expiration of twelve days

the

the Liquor will be fit for ufe. Touch the cheeks lightly with this Tincture, and it will fcarcely be poffible to perceive that rouge has been laid on, it will fo nearly refemble the natural bloom.

242. *An Oil that poffeffes the fame Property.*

TAKE ten pounds of Sweet Almonds, an ounce of Red Sanders in powder, and an ounce of bruifed Cloves; pour on them a gill of White Wine, and three quarters of a gill of Rofe-water; ftir them well every day. At the end of eight or nine days, fqueeze the pafte in a prefs in the fame manner as when you mean to extract Oil of Almonds.

SWEET-SCENTED BAGS.

243. *A sweet-scented Bag to wear in the Pocket.*

TAKE thin Perfian, and make it into little bags about four inches wide, in the form of an oblong fquare. Rub the infide lightly with a little Civet, then fill them with coarfe powder a la Marechale, or any other odoriferous Powder you choofe; to which add a few Cloves, with a little Yellow Sanders beaten fmall, and few up the mouths of the bags.

244. *Bags to fcent Linen.*

TAKE Rofe Leaves dried in the fhade, Cloves beat to a grofs powder, and Mace fcraped; mix them together, and put the compofition into little bags.

245. *An agreeable sweet-scented Composition.*

TAKE Florentine Orrice, a pound and a half; Rose Wood, six ounces; Calamus Aromaticus, half a pound; Yellow Sanders, a quarter of a pound; Gum Benjamin, five ounces; Cloves, half an ounce; and Cinnamon, an ounce: beat the whole into powder, and fill your bags with it.

246. *Ingredients for various Sorts of these little Bags or Satchels.*

FOR this purpose may be used different parts of the Aromatic Plants; as Leaves of Southernwood, Dragon-wort, Balm, Mint both garden and wild, Dittany, Ground-ivy, Bay, Hyssop, Lovage, Sweet Marjoram, Origanum, Pennyroyal, Thyme,

Rose-

Rosemary, Savory, Scordium, and Wild Thyme. The Flowers of the Orange, Lemon, Lime, and Citron Tree, Saffron, Lavender, Roses, Lily of the Valley, Clove-july-flower, Wall-flower, Jonquil, and Mace. Fruits, as Aniseeds, &c. The Rinds of Lemons, Oranges, &c. Small green Oranges, Juniper-berries, Nutmegs, and Cloves. Roots of Acorus, Bohemian Angelica, Oriental Costus, Sweet Flag, Orrice, Zedoary, &c. The Woods of Rhodium, Juniper, Caffia, St. Lucia, Sanders, &c. Gums, as Frankincense, Myrrh, Storax, Benjamin, Labdanum, Ambergrise, and Amber. Barks, as Canella Alba, Cinnamon, &c.

Care must be taken that all these ingredients are perfectly dry, and kept in a dry place. To prevent their turning black, add a little common Salt. When you

choose

choofe to have any particular Flower predominant, a greater quantity of that plant
muft be ufed in proportion to the other
ingredients.

W A S H - B A L L S.

247.   *White Soap.*

THIS foap is made with one part of the
Lees of Spanifh Pot-afh and Quick-lime,
to two parts of Oil of Olives or Oil of
Almonds.

248.   *Honey Soap.*

TAKE four ounces of White Soap, and
as much Honey, half an ounce of Salt
of Tartar, and two or three drachms of
the diftilled Water of Fumitory; mix the
whole together. This Soap cleanfes the

K 4   fkin

ſkin well, and renders it delicately white and ſmooth. It is alſo uſed advantageouſly, to efface the marks of burns and ſcalds.

249. *A perfumed Soap.*

TAKE four ounces of Marſh-mallow Roots ſkinned and dried in the ſhade, powder them, and add an ounce of Starch, the ſame quantity of Wheaten Flour, ſix drachms of freſh Pine-nut Kernels, two ounces of blanched Almonds, an ounce and a half of Orange Kernels huſked, two ounces of Oil of Tartar, the ſame quantity of Oil of Sweet Almonds, and thirty grains of Muſk: thoroughly incorporate the whole, and add to every ounce, half an ounce of Florentine Orriceroot in fine powder. Then ſteep half a pound of freſh Marſh-mallow Roots

bruiſed

bruifed in the diftilled Water of Mallows, or Orange Flowers, for twelve hours, and forcibly fqueezing out the liquor, make, with this mucilage, and the preceding Powders and Oils, a ftiff Pafte, which is to be dried in the fhade, and formed into round balls. Nothing exceeds this Soap for fmoothing the fkin, or rendering the hands delicately white.

250. *Fine fcented Wafh-ball.*

TAKE of the beft White Soap, half a pound, and fhave it into thin flices with a knife; then take two ounces and a half of Florentine Orrice, three quarters of an ounce of Calamus Aromaticus, and the fame quantity of Elder Flowers; of Cloves, and dried Rofe Leaves, each half an ounce; Coriander-feeds, Lavender, and Bay Leaves, of each a drachm, with three

K 5   drachms

drachms of Storax. Reduce the whole to fine powder, which knead into a Paste with the Soap; adding a few grains of Musk or Ambergrise. When you make this Paste into Wash-balls, soften it with a little Oil of Almonds to render the composition more lenient. Too much cannot be said in favour of this Wash-ball, with regard to its cleansing and cosmetic property.

251. *A Wash-ball, an excellent Cosmetic for the Face and Hands.*

TAKE a pound of Florentine Orrice, a quarter of a pound of Storax, two ounces of Yellow Sanders, half an ounce of Cloves, as much fine Cinnamon, a Nutmeg, and twelve grains of Ambergrise; beat the whole into very fine pow-and sift them through a lawn sieve, all ex-cept

cept the Ambergrife, which is to be added afterwards. Then take two pounds of the fineft White Soap, fhaved fmall, and infufe it in three pints of Brandy, four or five days. When it is diffolved, add a little Orange Flower-water, and knead the whole into a very ftiff Pafte with the beft Starch finely powdered. Then mix the Ambergrife, with a little Gum Tragacanth liquefied in fweet-fcented Water. Of this Pafte make Wafh-balls; dry them in the fhade, and polifh them with a Pafteboard or Lignum Vitæ cup.

252. *Bologna Wafh-balls.*

TAKE a pound of Italian Soap cut in fmall bits, and a quarter of a pound of Lime; pour on them two quarts of Brandy, let them ferment together twenty-four hours, then fpread the mafs on a fheet of

filtring

filtring paper to dry. When quite dry, beat it in a marble mortar, with half an ounce of St. Lucia Wood, an ounce and a half of Yellow Sanders, half an ounce of Orrice-root, and as much Calamus Aromaticus, all finely powdered. Knead the whole into a Paste with Whites of Eggs, and a quarter of a pound of Gum Tragacanth diffolved in Rofe-water, and then form it into Wafh-balls according to the ufual method.

264. *An excellent Wafh-ball for the Complexion.*

TAKE two ounces of Venetian Soap; diffolve it in two ounces of Lemon Juice, an ounce of Oil of Bitter Almonds, and the fame quantity of Oil of Tartar. Mix the whole together, and ftir the mixture till it acquires the confiftence of a thick Pafte.

254. *Seraglio Wash-balls.*

TAKE a pound of Florentine Orrice-roots, a quarter of a pound of Gum Benjamin, two ounces of Storax, two ounces of Yellow Sanders, half an ounce of Cloves, a drachm of Cinnamon, a little Lemon-peel, an ounce of St. Lucia Wood, and one Nutmeg. Reduce the whole to fine powder; then take about two pounds of White Soap fhaved thin, fteep it with the above Powder in three pints of Brandy, four or five days. Afterwards kneading the mafs with a fufficient quantity of Starch, and adding to it the Whites of Eggs, with Gum Tragacanth diffolved in fome odoriferous Water, form the Pafte into Wafh-balls of what fize you pleafe. A few grains of Mufk or Civet, or a little Effential Oil of Lavender, Bergamot, Rofes, Cloves, Clove-july-flowers,

6

flowers, Jasmine, Cinnamon, in short, any that best pleases the fancy of the person who prepares these Wash-balls, may be incorporated with the Paste while forming into a mass.

255. *A Hepatic Salt, to preserve the Complexion.*

TAKE Roots of Agrimony, two pounds; Roots of Succory and Scorzonera, of each a pound; Bitter Costus and Turmeric, of each half a pound; Calamus Aromaticus and Rhapontic, of each a quarter of a pound; Wormwood, Southernwood, Sweet Maudlin, Harts-tongue, Fluellin, Liverwort, Fumitory, and Dodder of Thyme, of each three ounces; calcine the whole in a reverberatory furnace, and add Ashes of Rhubarb and Cassia Lignea of each an ounce and a half. Make a lee with these Ashes in a decoction of the Flowers of

Liverwort,

Liverwort, and extract the Salt according to art. This Salt caufes the bile to flow freely, removes obftructions, cures the jaundice, takes away a fallow complexion, and imparts to the fkin the ruddy vermillion bloom of health. Its dofe is from twenty-four to thirty-fix grains, in any convenient vehicle.

EYE-BROWS.

256. *To change the Eye-brows black.*

RUB them frequently with ripe Elderberries. Some ufe burnt Cork, or Cloves burnt in the candle; others prefer the Black of Frankincenfe, Rofin, and Maftic. This Black will not melt nor come off by fweating.

MARKS OF THE SKIN.

257.   *To efface Spots or Marks of the Mother,*
on any Part of the Body.

Steep in Vinegar of Rofes, or ftrong White Wine Vinegar, Borrage Roots ftripped of their fmall adhering fibres, and let them ftand to infufe twelve or fourteen hours. Bathe the part affected frequently with this Infufion, and in time the marks will totally difappear.

268. *Or,*

Take, towards the end of the month of May, the Roots and Leaves of the herb Bennet; diftil them with a fufficient quantity of Water in an alembic, and frequently foment the marks with the diftilled Water.

259. *To take away Marks, and fill up the Cavities left after the Small-Pox.*

TAKE Oil of the four larger Cold Seeds, Oil of Eggs, and Oil of Sweet Almonds, of each half an ounce; Plantain and Night-shade Water, of each three quarters of an ounce; Litharge and Cerufs finely pow-dered and wafhed in Rofe-water, of each a drachm. Put the Litharge and Cerufs into a brafs pot, and incorporate them over a fire, with the Oils, adding the latter gradually, and ftirring the mixture all the while. Then add by degrees alfo the Nightfhade and Plantain Water, and thus form a Liniment, with which anoint the face of the patient as foon as the fcabs of the Small-pox begin to fcale off; and repeat the application as occafion may require.

COMPLEXION.

260. *Certain Methods to improve the Complexion.*

BROWN ladies fhould frequently bathe themfelves, and wafh their faces with a few drops of Spirit of Wine, fometimes with Virgin's Milk, and the diftilled Waters of Pimpernel, White Tanfy, Bean Flowers, &c. Thefe deterfive penetrating applications, by degrees remove the kind of varnifh that covers the fkin, and thus render more free the perfpiration, which is the only real cofmetic.

261. *The Montpellier Toilet.*

FOR this purpofe a new light-woven linen cloth muft be procured, and cut of a proper fize to make a toilet. The firft

ftep

ftep you take muft be to wafh the cloth
perfectly clean in feveral different Waters,
then fpread it out to dry, and afterwards
fteep it twenty-four hours in Sweet-fcented
Water, viz. half Angelic, and half Rofe-
water. On removing the cloth out of the
water, gently fqueeze it, and hang it up to
dry in the open air. Then lay on it the
following compofition.

TAKE dried Orange Flowers, Roots of
Elecampane, and Florentine Orrice, of
each half a pound; of Yellow Sanders,
four ounces ; of the Marc or Refiduum of
Angelic Water, two ounces; of Rofe-
wood and Sweet Flag, each an ounce; of
Gum Labdanum, Calamus Aromaticus,
and Cloves, each half an ounce ; of Cinnamon, two drachms; beat all thefe ingredients into powder, and make them into
a Pafte with Mucilage of Gum Tragacanth

diffolved

diffolved in Angelic Water. Rub this
Pafte hard on both fides of your cloth,
leaving on it the little bits that may adhere, becaufe they render the furface
more fmooth. Afterwards hang up the
cloth, and when half dry, again rub both
fides, with a fponge wetted with Angelic
Water, to render the cloth yet more
fmooth ; after which dry it thoroughly,
and fo'd it up. This cloth is generally
lined with taffety, and covered with fattin,
and is never enclofed within more than
two pieces of fome kind of thin filk, as
Taffety, &c.

262. *Sweet-fcented Troches to correct a
bad Breath.*

TAKE Frankincenfe, a fcruple ; Amber-
grife, fifteen grains ; Mufk, feven grains ;
Oil of Lemons, fix drops ; double refined
Sugar,

Sugar, an ounce. Form thefe ingredients
into little Troches with Mucilage of Gum
Arabic, made with Cinnamon Water.
Hold one or two in the mouth as often
occafion requires.

263. *A curious Varnifh for the Face.*

FILL into a bottle three quarters of a
pint of good Brandy, infufing in it an
ounce of Gum Sandarach, and half an
ounce of Gum Benjamin. Frequently
fhake the bottle till the Gums are wholly
diffolved, and then let it ftand to fettle.

Apply this varnifh after having wafhed
the face clean, and it will give the fkin
the fineft luftre imaginable.

WARTS.

264. *A Medicine to cure Warts.*

TAKE the Leaves of Campanula, bruife them, and rub them upon the warts. Repeat this operation three or four times, if they prove obftinate; and they will afterwards foon wafte away without leaving the leaft mark behind. This plant perhaps is not to be met with every where, but Botanifts have defcribed it by the following marks. Its leaves, fay they, refemble thofe of the Blue Bell Flower, or Ivy, are ftringy, compofed of five lobes, without down, are fmall at the end, and have a loofe flabby ftalk.

265. *Another.*

TAKE the inner Rind of a Lemon, fteep it four and twenty hours in diftilled Vinegar,

gar, and apply it to the warts. It muſt not be left on the part above three hours at a time, and is to be applied afreſh every day.

266. *Or,*

DIVIDE a Red Onion, and rub the warts well with it.

267. *Or,*

ANOINT the warts with the milky Juice of the herb Mercury ſeveral times, and they will gradually waſte away.

268. *Another ſafe and experienced Method.*

RUB the warts with a pared Pippin, and a few days afterwards they will be found to diſappear.

VINEGARS.

269. *Diſtilled Vinegar.*

FILL a ſtone cucurbit about three parts and a half full of White Wine Vinegar; place the veſſel in a furnace ſo contrived as to contain three parts of the height of the cucurbit; mould the openings that remain between the ſides and the upper part of the veſſel with clay tempered with water; lute the veſſel, fix on a receiver, and begin your diſtillation with a moderate fire, which is to be increaſed by degrees till about five ſixths of the Vinegar are drawn off, which is called Diſtilled Vinegar. A ſmall quantity of acid Liquor ſtill remains in the cucurbit of the conſiſtence of Honey; which if you think proper may be dried hard by the aſſiſtance of a vapour-bath. The Vinegar diſtilled

from

from this fubftance is infinitely more acid, than that which was drawn off by the firft procefs.

To rectify diftilled Vinegar, put it into a clean veffel, fetting it in the fame degree of fire as at firft to feparate more phlegm, and in every thing proceed as before, till the bottom is almoft dry. Neither the fire nor diftillation however muft be urged too far, for fear of giving an empyreumatic flavour to that which is already diftilled.

Diftilled Vinegar is ufed externally, mixed with Water, to wafh the face : it is cooling, and takes away the troublefome little pimples that fometimes affect this part.

270. *Diftilled* Lavender *Vinegar.*

PUT into a ftone cucurbit any quantity of frefh-gathered Lavender Flowers picked

L   clean

clean from the Stalks; pour on them as much diftilled Vinegar as is requifite to make the Flowers float; diftil in a vapour-bath, and draw off about three fourths of the Vinegar.

In the fame manner are prepared the Vinegars from all other vegetable fub-ftances. Compound Vinegars are made by mixing feveral aromatic fubftances together; obferving only to bruife all hard woody ingredients, and to let them infufe a fufficient time in the Vinegar before you proceed to diftillation.

Lavender Vinegar is of ufe for the Toilet; it is cooling, and when applied to the face, braces up the relaxed fibres of the fkin.

271. *Vinegar of the Four Thieves.*

TAKE of the tops of Sea and Roman Wormwood, Rosemary, Sage, Mint and Rue, of each an ounce and a half; Lavender Flowers two ounces, Calamus Aromaticus, Cinnamon, Cloves, Nutmeg, and Garlic, of each a quarter of an ounce; Camphire, half an ounce; Red Wine Vinegar, a gallon. Choose all the foregoing ingredients dry, except the Garlic and Camphire; beat them into grofs powder, and cut the Garlic into thin flices; put the whole into a matrafs; pour the Vinegar on them, and digeſt the mixture in the fun, or in a gentle fand-heat, for three weeks or a month. Then ſtrain off the Vinegar by expreſſion, filter it through paper, and add the Camphire diſſolved in a little rectified Spirit of Wine. Keep it for ufe in a bottle, tightly corked.

The

The Vinegar of the Four Thieves is antipeftilential, and is ufed fuccefsfully as a prefervative againft contagious diforders. The hands and face are wafhed with it every day; the room fumigated with it, as are alfo the cloaths, in order to fecure the perfon from infection.

EYES.

272. *To cure watery Eyes.*

PREPARE a decoction with the Leaves of Betony, Fennel Roots, and a little fine Frankincenfe, which ufe as an Eye-water.

273. *Or,*

FREQUENTLY bathe the Eyes with a decoction of Chervil.

274. *Or,*

DROP into the Eyes now and then a little Juice of Rue, mixed with clarified Honey.

275. *An excellent Ophthalmic Lotion.*

TAKE White Vitriol and Bay Salt, of each an ounce; decrepitate them together, and when the detonation is over, pour on them, in an earthen pan, a pint of boiling Water or Rofe-water. Stir them together, and let them ftand fome hours. A varioufly coloured fkin will be formed on the furface, which carefully fkim off, and put the clear liquor into a bottle for. ufe.

This was communicated to the author as a great fecret; and indeed he has found it by experience very fafely to cool

L 3 and

and repel thofe fharp humours that fometimes fall upon the Eyes, and to clear the
latter of beginning films and fpecks. If
too fharp, it may be diluted with a little
Rofe-water.

276. *An Ophthalmic Poultice.*

TAKE half a pint of Alum Curd, and
mix with it a fufficient quantity of Red
Rofe Leaves powdered, to give it a proper
confiftence. This is an excellent application for fore moift eyes, and admirably
cools and reprefses defluxions.

277. *A Poultice for inflamed Eyes.*

TAKE half a pint of a decoction of
Linfeed in Water, and as much Flour of
Linfeed as is fufficient to make it of a
proper confiftence. This Poultice is preferable to a Bread and Milk Poultice for
inflamed Eyes, as it will not grow four
and acrid.

278. *Sir Hans Sloane's Eye Salve.*

TAKE prepared Tutty, one ounce; prepared Bloodstone, two scruples; Aloes in fine powder, twelve grains; mix them well together in a marble mortar, with as much Viper's Fat as is requisite to bring the whole to the consistence of a soft salve. It is to be applied with a hair pencil, the eyes winking or a little opened. It has cured many whose eyes were covered with opake films and scabs, left by preceding disorders of those parts.

279. *An Ophthalmic Fomentation.*

TAKE three quarters of an ounce of White Poppy Heads bruised with their Seeds, and boil them in Milk and Water, of each half a pint, till one half is wasted away; then dissolve in the strained Li-

L 4

quor

quor a fcruple of Sugar of Lead. This is an excellent application for moift, or inflamed Eyes.

280. *A fimple Remedy to ftrengthen the Sight.*

SNUFF up the Juice of Eyebright, and drop a little into the eyes. It not only clears and ftrengthen the fight, but takes off all fpecks, films, mifts, or fuffufions.

Herb Snuffs are alfo excellent to ftrengthen and preferve the fight; various Receips for making which will afterwards be given.

SUPPLEMENT.

Manner of taking out all Kinds of Spots and Stains from Linen and Stuffs; and various other useful Receipts.

281. *To take Iron Mould out of Linen.*

Hold the Iron Mould over the Fume of Boiling Water for some time, then pour on the spot a little Juice of Sorrel and a little Salt, and when the cloth has thoroughly imbibed the Juice, wash it in Lee.

282. *To take out Stains of Oil.*

Take Windsor Soap shaved thin, put it into a bottle half full of Lee, throw in the size of a Nut of Sal Armoniac, a little Cabbage Juice, two Yolks of new-laid Eggs, and Ox-gall at discretion, and lastly an ounce of powdered Tartar: then cork

L 5

the

the bottle, and expofe it to the heat of
the noon-day fun four days, at the expiration of which time it becomes fit for
ufe.   Pour this Liquor on the ftains, and
rub it well on both fides of the cloth;
then wafh the ftains with clear Water, or
rather with the following foap, and when
the cloth is dry, they will no longer
appear.

283. *Scouvering Balls.*

TAKE foft Soap, or Fuller's Earth; mix
it with Vine Afhes fifted through a fine
fieve, and with powdered Chalk, Alum, and
Tartar, of each equal parts; form the mafs
into balls, which dry in the fhade.   Their
ufe is to rub on fpots and ftains, wafhing
the fpotted part afterwards in clear Water.

284. *To take out Stains of Coomb.*

PUT Butter on the ftain, and rub it
well with a piece of brown paper laid on
a heated filver fpoon; then wafh the
whole

whole in the same manner as directed for spots of Wax.

285. *To take out Stains of Urine.*

WASH the stained place well with boiled Urine, and afterwards wash it in clear Water.

286. *To take out Stains on Cloth of whatever Colour.*

TAKE half a pound of Honey, the size of a Nut of Sal Armoniac, and the Yolk of an Egg; mix them together, and put a little of this mixture on the stain, letting it remain till dry. Then wash the cloth with fair Water, and the stains will disappear. Water impregnated with mineral Alkaline Salt or Soda, Ox-gall, and Black Soap, is also very good to take out spots of grease.

287. *To take out Spots of Ink.*

As soon as the accident happens, wet the place with Juice of Sorrel, or Lemon,

or

or with Vinegar, and the beſt hard White
Soap.

288.   *To take out Spots of Pitch and Tur-*
pentine.

Pour a good deal of Sallad Oil on the
ſtained place, and let it dry on it four and
twenty hours; then rub the inſide of the
cloth with the Scowring Ball and warm
Water.

289.   *To take out Spots of Oil on Sattin and*
other Stuffs, and on Paper.

If the ſpot be not of long ſtanding,
take the Aſhes of Sheep's Trotters calcined,
and apply them hot both under and upon
the ſpot.   Lay on it ſomething heavy, letting it remain all night; and if in the
morning the ſpot is not entirely effaced,
renew the application repeatedly till it
wholly diſappear.

290. *To take out Spots on Silk.*

RUB the Spots with Spirit of Turpentine; this Spirit exhaling, carries off with it the Oil that caufes the Spot.

291. *Balls to take out Stains.*

TAKE an ounce of Quick-lime, half a pound of Soap, and a quarter of a pound of White Clay; moiften the whole with Water, and make it into little balls, with which rub the ftains, and afterwards wafh them with fair water.

292. *To clean Gold and Silver Lace.*

TAKE the Gall of an Ox and of a Pike, mixed well together in fair Water, and rub the gold or filver with this compofition.

293. *To reftore to Tapeftry its original Luftre.*

SHAKE well, and thoroughly clean the tapeftry; then rub it twice over with

Chalk,

Chalk, which, after remaining feven or eight hours each time, is to be brufhed off with a hard brufh; the tapeftry being like-wife well beaten with a ftick, and fhaked.

294.   *To clean Turkey Carpets.*

To revive the colour of a Turkey Car-pet, beat it well with a ftick, till the duft is all got out; then with Lemon or Sorrel Juice take out the fpots of ink, if the car-pet be ftained with any; wafh it in cold Water, and afterwards fhake out all the Water from the threads of the carpet. When it is thoroughly dry, rub it all over with the Crumb of a hot Wheaten Loaf; and if the weather is very fine, hang it out in the open air a night or two.

295.   *To refresh Tapestry, Carpets, Hangings,*
or Chairs.

BEAT the duft out of them on a dry day as clean as poffible, and brufh them well

well with a dry brush. Afterwards rub them well over with a good lather of Castile Soap, laid on with a brush. Wash off the froth with common Water; then wash the tapestry, &c. with Alum Water. When the cloth is dry, you will find most of the colours restored. Those that are yet too faint, touch up with a pencil dipped in suitable colours, and indeed you may run over the whole piece in the same manner with water colours, mixed with weak gum water, and, if well done, it will cause the tapestry, &c. to look at a distance like new.

296. *To take Wax out of Silk or Camblet.*

TAKE Soft Soap, rub it well on the spots of wax, dry it in the sun till it grows very hot, then wash the spotted part with cold Water, and the wax will be entirely taken out.

297. *To take Wax out of Velvet of all Colours except Crimson.*

TAKE a Crummy Wheaten Loaf, cut it in two, toaſt it before the fire, and while very hot, apply it to the part ſpotted with wax. Then apply another piece of toaſted Bread hot as before, and continue to repeat this application till the wax is entirely taken out.

299. *To waſh Gold or Silver Work on Linen, or any other Stuff, ſo as to look like new.*

TAKE a pound of Ox-gall; Honey and Soap, of each three ounces; Florentine Orrice in fine powder, three ounces; mix the whole in a glaſs veſſel into a Paſte, and expoſe it to the ſun during ten days; then make a decoction of Bran, and ſtrain it clear. Plaſter over with your bitter Paſte, the places you want to clean, and after-

afterwards wafh off the Pafte with the Bran-water, till the latter is no longer tinged. Then wipe with a clean linen cloth the places you have wafhed; cover them with a clean napkin, dry them in the fun, prefs and glaze, and the work will look as well as when new.

299. *To take Spots out of Silken or Woollen Stuffs.*

TAKE a fufficient quantity of the fineft Starch, wet it in an earthen pipkin with Brandy, rub a little on the fpots, let it dry on them, and then brufh it off; repeat this operation till the fpots are wholly taken out. You muft be careful to beat and brufh well the place on which the Starch was applied.

300. *To take Stains of Oil out of Cloth.*

TAKE Oil of Tartar, pour a little on the fpot, immediately wafh the place with

warm

warm Water, and two or three times after with cold Water, and the fpot will entirely difappear.

301.   To take Stains out of White Cloth.

Boil an ounce of Alum in a gallon and a half of Water, for half an hour, then add a piece of White Soap, and half a ounce more of Alum, and after it has ftood in cold infufion two days, wafh with this mixture ftains in any kind of white cloth.

302.   To take Stains out of Crimfon Velvet, and coloured Velvets.

Take a quart of ftrong Lee made with Vine Afhes, diffolve in it half an ounce of Alum; and when the mixture has fettled, ftrain it through a linen cloth. Then take half a drachm of foft Soap, and the fame quantity of Caftile Soap, a drachm of Alum, half a drachm of Crude Sal Armoniac,

niac, a fcruple of common Salt, a little
Loaf Sugar, Juice of Celandine, and the
Gall of a Calf; mix the whole well, and
ftrain off the Liquor. When you want to
ufe it, take a little Brazil Wood Shavings
with fome Scarlet Flocks, boil them in
this Liquor, and when ftrained off, it will
be very good to take fpots or ftains out of
crimfon velvet or cloth. For velvets or
cloths of other colours, you dye your Liquor of the proper colour, by boiling in it
fome Flocks of the fame colour as the
cloth you intend to clean.

303. *A Soap that takes out all manner of*
Spots and Stains.

TAKE the Yolks of fix Eggs, half a
table fpoonful of bruifed Salt, and a pound
of Venetian Soap; mix the whole together
with the Juice of Beet-roots, and form
it into round balls, that are to be dried in
the

the fhade. The method of ufing this Soap
is to wet with fair Water the ftained part
of the cloth, and rub both fides of it well
with this Soap; then wafh the cloth in
Water, and the ftain will no longer appear.

304. *Another Method to take Spots or Stains*
  out of White Silk or Crimfon Velvet.

FIRST foak the place well with Brandy
or Spirit of Wine, then rub it over with
the White of a new-laid Egg, and dry
it in the fun. Wafh it brifkly in cold
Water, rubbing the place where the
fpot is, hard between the fingers; and repeat this operation a fecond and even a
third time, if it has not previoufly fuc-
ceeded.

305. *A Receipt to clean Gloves without*
  wetting.

LAY the Gloves upon a clean board,
and mix together Fuller's Earth and
Powder

Powder of Alum very dry, which lay over them on both fides with a moderately ftiff brufh. Then fweep off the Powder, fprinkle them well with Bran and Whiting, and duft them thoroughly. If not very greafy, this will render them as clean as when new; but if they are extremely greafy, rub them with ftale Crumb of Bread, and Powder of burnt Bones, then pafs them over with a woollen Cloth dipped in Fuller's Earth or Alum Powder.

306. *To colour Gloves.*

IF you want to colour them of a dark colour, take Spanifh Brown and Black Earth; if lighter, Yellow Ochre and Whiting, and fo of the reft; mix the colour with Size of a moderate ftrength, then wet the Gloves over with the Colour, and hang them to dry gradually. Beat out the fuperfluous Colour, fmooth them over with a fleeking ftick, and reduce them to a proper fize.

307. *To wash Point Lace.*

DRAW the Lace pretty tight in a frame, then with a lather of Caſtile Soap a little warm, rub it over gently by means of a fine bruſh. When you perceive it clean on one ſide, turn it, and rub the other in the ſame manner; then throw over the Lace ſome Alum-water, taking off the Suds, and with ſome thin Starch ge over the wrong ſide of the Lace; iron it on the ſame ſide when dry, and raiſe the flowers with a bodkin.

308. *To clean Point Lace without waſhing.*

FIX the lace in a frame, and rub it with Crumb of ſtale Bread, which afterwards duſt out.

309. *To waſh black and white Sarcenet.*

LAY the ſilk ſmooth upon a board, ſpread a little Soap over the dirty places,

make

make a lather with Caſtile Soap, and with a fine bruſh dipped in it, paſs over the ſilk the right way, viz. lengthways, and continue ſo to do till that ſide is ſufficiently ſcowered. Then turn the ſilk, ſcower the other ſide in the ſame manner, and put the ſilk into boiling Water, where it muſt lie ſome time; afterwards rince it in thin Gum Water; if white ſilk, add a little Smalt. This being done, fold the ſilk, clapping or preſſing out the water with your hands on a dry Carpet, till it become tolerably dry; if white, dry it over the Smoak of Brimſtone till ready for ſmoothing, which is to be done on the right ſide with an Iron moderately hot.

310. *A Soap to take out all Kinds of Stains.*

BOIL a handful of Strawberries or Strawberry Leaves in a quart of Water and a pint of Vinegar, adding two pounds of Caſtile

Caftile Soap, and half a pound of Chalk in fine powder; boil them together till the water has evaporated. When you ufe it, wet the place with the fharpeft Vinegar or Verjuice, and rub it over with this Soap; dry it afterwards before the fire or in the fun.

311. *An expeditious Method to take Stains out of Scarlet, or Velvet of any other Colour.*

TAKE Soapwort, when bruifed ftrain out its Juice, and add to it a fmall quantity of black Soap. Wafh the Stain with this Liquor, fuffering it to dry between whiles; and by this means, in a day or two the Spots will difappear.

DIFFERENT WAYS OF PREPARING SNUFF.

312. *Method of making Snuff.*

FIRST ftrip off the Stalks and large fibres of the Tobacco, then fpread the

Leaves

I

Leaves on a mat or carpet to dry in the
fun, afterwards rub them in a mortar, and
fift the powder through a coarfe or fine
fieve, according to the degree of finenefs
you would have your fnuff; or grind the
Tobacco Leaves, prepared in the manner before directed, in a fnuff-mill, either
into a grofs or fine powder, according as
you prefs clofe or eafe the mill-ftone.

313. *Method of cleanfing Snuff in order to
feent it.*

Fix a thick linen cloth in a little
tub that has a hole in the bottom,
ftopped with a plug that can eafily be
taken out, to let the water run off when
wanted. This cloth muft cover the whole
infide of the tub, and be faftened all round
the rim. Put your Snuff in it, and pour
on the Water. When it has been fteeped
twenty-four hours, let the Water run out,

M and

and pour on frefh; repeat this operation three times, if you would have the Snuff thoroughly cleanfed, and every time fqueeze the Snuff hard in the cloth, to difcharge the Water entirely from it. Then place your Snuff on an ozier hurdle covered with a thick linen cloth, and let it dry in the fun; when it is thoroughly dry, put it again into the tub, with a fufficient quantity of Angelic, Orange Flower, or Rofe-water. At the expiration of twenty-four hours take the Snuff out of the water, and dry it as before, frequently ftirring it about, and fprinkling it with the fame fweet-fcented Water as was ufed at firft. The whole of this preparation is abfolutely neceffary to render Snuff fit to receive the fcent of Flowers.

If the Snuff is not required to be of a very excellent quality, and you are unwilling

ling to waste more of it than can possibly
be avoided, wash it only once, and slightly
cleanse it.. This purgation may the
better suffice, if while drying in the sun,
you take care. to knead the Snuff into a
cake several times, and often sprinkle it
with some sweet-scented Water.

314. *Method of scenting Snuff.*

THE Flowers that most readily communicate their flavour to Snuff are Orange Flowers, Jasmine, Musk Roses, and Tuberoses.
You must procure a box lined with dry
white paper; in this strow your Snuff on
the bottom about the thickness of an inch,
over which place a thin layer of Flowers,
then another layer of Snuff, and continue
to lay your Flowers and Snuff alternately
in this manner, until the box is full. After
they have lain together four and twenty
hours, sift your Snuff through a sieve to

M 2 separate

feparate it from the Flowers, which are to be thrown away, and frefh ones applied in their room in the former method. Continue to do this till the Snuff is fufficiently fcented; then put it into a canifter, which keep clofe ftopped.

215. *Or,*

Put your Flowers that are placed over each layer of the Snuff, between two pieces of white paper pricked full of holes with a large pin, and fift through a fieve the Snuff that may happen to get between the papers. To fcent the Snuff perfectly it is neceffary to renew the Flowers four or five times. This method is the leaft troublefome of the two.

A very agreeable fcented Snuff may be made with Rofes, by taking Rofe-buds, ftripping off the green cup, and

piftil

piftil that rifes in the middle, and fixing in its place a Clove; being careful not to feparate the Leaves that are clofed together. The Rofe-buds thus prepared, are to be expofed to the heat of the fun a whole month, inclofed in a glafs well ftopped, and are then fit for ufe.

To make Snuff fcented with a thoufand Flowers, take a number of different Flow-ers, and mix them together, proportioning the quantity of each Flower, to the degree of its perfume, fo that the flavour of no one particular Flower may be predominant.

316. *Perfumed Snuff.*

TAKE fome Snuff, and rub it in your hands with a little Civet, opening the body of the Civet ftill more by rubbing it in your hands with frefh Snuff; and when you have mixed it perfectly with the Snuff,

put

put them into a canister. Snuff is flavoured with other perfumes in the fame way.

317. *Or,*

PERFUME your Snuff by mixing it well with the hands, in a heated iron or brafs mortar, befmeared with a few grains of Ambergrife.

318. *Snuff after the Maltefe Fafhion.*

PERFUME with Ambergrife, in the manner already defcribed, fome Snuff previoufly fcented with Orange Flowers. Then grind in a mortar a little Sugar with about ten grains of Civet, and mix by little and little with about a pound of the foregoing Snuff.

319. *The Genuine Maltefe Snuff.*

TAKE Roots of Liquorice, and Roots of the Rofe-bufh, peel off their outer fkin, dry them, powder them, and fift the

powder

powder through a fine fieve, then fcent them according to your fancy, or in the fame manner as French Snuff, adding a little White **Wine,** Brandy, or a very little Spirit of **Wine,** and rubbing the Snuff well between your hands.

320. *Italian Snuff.*

Put into a mortar, or other convenient veffel, a quantity of Snuff already fcented with fome Flower, pour on it a little White Wine, and add, if agreeable, fome Effence of Ambergrife, Mufk, or any other Perfume you like beft ; ftir the Snuff and rub it well between your hands.   Scent Snuff in this manner with any particular flavour, and put the different fcented Snuffs in feparate boxes, which are to be marked, to prevent miftakes.

321. *Snuff fcented after the Spanifh Manner.*

Take a lump of double-refined Sugar, rub it in a mortar with twenty grains of Mufk ;

Mufk ; add by little and little a pound of Snuff, and grind the whole with ten grains of Civet, rubbing it afterwards well between your hands..

Seville Snuff is fcented with twenty grains of Vanilloes only. Keep your Snuff in canifters clofely ftopped, to prevent the fcent from exhaling.

As Spanifh Snuff is very fine and of a reddifh colour, to imitate it nicely, take the beft Dutch Snuff, well cleanfed, granulated, and coloured red; beat it fine, and fift it through a very fine lawn fieve. After it has been cleanfed according to the foregoing directions, it is fit to take any fcent whatever.

There is no rifk in ufing a fieve that retains the fcent of any Flower, to perfume your Snuff with the flavour of Mufk,

Amber-

Ambergrife, or any other Perfume. On the contrary, the Snuff receives the Perfume the more readily, and preferves its flavour the longer on that account.

322. *Method of dying Snuff Red or Yellow.*

TAKE the fize of a nut or two of Yellow or Red Ochre, and to temper the colour mix with it a little White Chalk. Grind thefe colours on a marble, with a little lefs than half an ounce of Oil of Sweet Almonds, and moiften with as much Water as the colour will take up, till it becomes a fmooth Pafte. Then mix it with a thin Mucilage of Gum Tragacanth to a proper confiftence, and put it into an earthen difh, ftirring into it about a pint more of Water. Aftewards take any quantity of cleanfed Snuff you pleafe, throw it upon the colour, and rub it well between your hands. When the Pafte is thoroughly

tinged

tinged with the colour, leave it till next morning to fettle, then fpread it thin on a cloth to dry, and place it in the fun, ftirring it about every now and then that it may dry equally. When dry, gum it with a very thin Mucilage of Gum Tragacanth made with fome fweet-fcented Water. To gum the Snuff as equally as poffible, wet the palms of your hands with this Gum Water, and rub the Snuff well between them. Afterwards dry it in the fun, and fift the colour that does not adhere to it through a very fine fieve. The Snuff is then properly prepared to receive any flavour you choofe.

323. *Herb Snuff.*

TAKE Sweet Marjoram, Marum Syriacum Leaves, and Lavender Flowers dried, of each half an ounce, Afarabacca Leaves, a drachm. Rub them all into a powder.

324. *Or,*

TAKE Betony Leaves and Marjoram, of each half an ounce; Afarabacca Leaves, a drachm. Beat them together into a powder.

325. *Or,*

TAKE Marjoram, Rofemary Flowers, Betony, and Flowers of Lilies of the Valley, of each a quarter of an ounce; Nutmegs, a drachm and a half; Volatile Salt, forty drops. Powder, and keep the mixture in a phial, clofe ftopped.

326. *Or,*

TAKE Flowers of Lavender, and Clove-july-flowers, of each a quarter of an ounce; Lilies of the Valley, Tiel-tree Flowers, Flowers of Sage, Betony, Rofemary, and Tops of Marjoram, of each half a drachm;

7   Cin-

Cinnamon, Aloes-wood, Yellow Sanders, and White Helebore-root, of each a drachm; Oil of Nutmegs and Oil of Lemon, of each three drops; mix them into a powder.

A pinch or two of any of these Snuffs may be taken night and morning medicinally, or at any time for pleasure. Used externally, they are serviceable for weak eyes and many disorders of the organs of sight and hearing. They also relieve head-aches, giddiness, palsies, lethargies, besides a variety of other complaints; and are, though agreeable and simple, far superior to what is sold under the name of Herb Snuff.

FINIS.

www.ingramcontent.com/pod-product-compliance
Lightning Source LLC
Chambersburg PA
CBHW030346270326
41926CB00009B/979